Child Studies

Child Studies

Child Care and Development from birth to seven years
– a two-year course

Tusia Werner

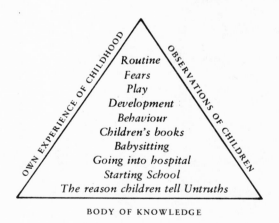

BODY OF KNOWLEDGE

Batsford Academic and Educational London

First published 1984

All rights reserved. No part of this publication
may be reproduced, in any form or by any means,
without permission from the Publisher

Typeset by Servis Filmsetting Ltd, Manchester
and printed in Great Britain by
Biddles Ltd
Guildford and Kings Lynn
for the publishers
Batsford Academic and Educational
an imprint of B T Batsford Ltd
4 Fitzhardinge Street
London W1H 0AH

British Library Cataloguing in Publication Data
Werner, Tusia
    Child studies.
    1. Child rearing
    I. Title
    649'.1   HQ769

ISBN 0 7134 4310 3

Contents

Acknowledgment

I would like to thank:

My pupils at Stanley Deason High School from whom I have learned so much, particularly the pupils whose contributions I have included in this book.

Linda Sandey for the drawings in Part I.

My two sons, Nick and Ben, for surviving my parenting mistakes.

My husband, John, who encouraged me to write this book.

T.W.
Brighton 1984

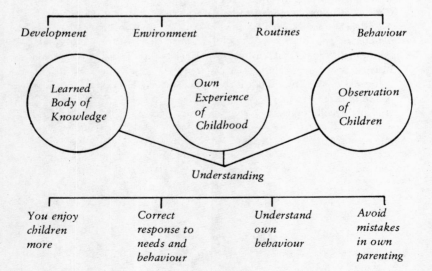

Introduction

The importance of education for family life and parenting has been emphasised by both Government and Her Majesty's Inspectors. GCE, as well as CSE, now have examination syllabuses encouraging these life skills.

This book, as well as developing confidence, encourages a sense of awe and wonder at the miracle of creation and the uniqueness of each individual.

The subject, so often dealt with in a female-orientated manner, is approached in such a way as to be equally appropriate to both sexes.

Pupils in the 14 to 16 age group are in many ways at the ideal age to study young children. It is a transition stage for them and in their search for their own identity they are responsive and interested in any subject which they see as being relevant. It becomes evident that a study of the body of knowledge about children, an analytical recall of their own childhood, together with close observation of young children in a variety of situations, enables the young adults to apply the knowledge they have acquired with confidence and success in real-life situations. They are able to respond with heightened enjoyment and appreciation not only to the relationships within their own families, ie with parents and younger siblings, but also to the many encounters they have with children when they are functioning as a babysitter, waitress, shop assistant, nurse, teacher or receptionist, as well as during casual everyday situations. The other implication is for parenthood – that when they become parents they will start with a positive attitude which will help them cope with the feelings of hostility children can provoke, rather than lashing out at the child in fury and frustration.

Teaching approach

This subject touches on the personal experience of pupils and their families and therefore can have unexpected repercussions. When dealing with this sort of material the teacher should avoid making the subject too personal by exposing pupils' experiences as these can be very painful; it is a good idea to impose an impersonal structure on discussion and written work, which serves to distance the impact.

Discussion techniques

In order to discuss a subject pupils need an input of information. Only then will the discussion be meaningful; recognising the implication of information to a

9

situation or a person. They should always be encouraged to support personal questions with information, observation and experience.

Whole class discussions This is where the teacher and the class interchange ideas. The teacher can either ask for voluntary contributions or ask each pupil to make a point. To avoid one or two pupils dominating a discussion the teacher can ask all the pupils to jot down points that occur to them.

Teacher's role In this type of discussion the teacher puts forward discussion topics, extends pupils' contributions by comments or asking further questions to stimulate ideas, reminding them to support their arguments with facts or observations and, of course, summing up the ideas put forward.

Group discussion This should include groups of four to six pupils. The selection of groups could be based on pupils' own choice or, alternatively, can be selected by the teacher. Each group can discuss the same topic, choosing different aspects from a selected theme or they can discuss different topics. It is useful to set a time limit that requires pupils to record main points raised in their group. A spokesman from each group can report to the whole class. Pupils can also record points made in order of importance. The teacher's role in this kind of discussion is to go round each group to help guide discussion. The points brought out during the lesson can be extended into some form of written work, with the teacher supplying the paragraph headings.

It is important for pupils to experience discussion as part of a learning programme but many pupils prefer the privacy offered by writing, so they can express their opinions or record their experiences. For the uninhibited pupil who is quite happy to voice opinion to the whole group, keeping a record of topics discussed, provides a good discipline and encourages thinking on paper as well as spoken thought.

Classroom requirements

There should be visual evidence in the classroom where the study takes place.

Display Paintings by young children (acquired from local nursery and first schools) showing the development of children as seen from their paintings and drawings.

Toys Examples of suitable toys for different age groups as well as a good selection of children's books. A sand tray and water trough are important as they provide absorbing play possibilities to any visiting children. Ideally the teaching room should be suitable for a small playgroup. A wendy house and a small climbing frame are valuable assets.

Classroom arrangements for the different needs of this subject Desks grouped to seat six can be placed near the corners of the room leaving free space in the centre of the room. When doing written work, research or group discussion, pupils can work at their desks.

Chairs can be positioned in a circle in the central free space and where sand, water and other toys can be placed when children come to the class with their mothers. This also provides an informal atmosphere when visiting speakers are invited.

When having a class discussion or receiving instruction, pupils can bring their chairs close to the teacher's desk. This compact grouping helps their concentration and encourages participation.

Viewing or listening preparation

It is advisable that the teacher should view or listen to each programme which has been recorded on video or tape *before* it is played to the pupils. It is a good idea to give the pupils an outline of what they are to hear and see in the programme, as well as emphasising any particular points of interest. This will serve to focus their attention as without such guidance many pupils will miss vital points. Sometimes it is a good idea to stop a programme at certain relevant places so pupils can make notes and comments or for the teacher to ask questions.

Watching television is an intimate experience and the pupils are best close to the set, in a huddle, rather than scattered about a classroom.

Observing children

The objectives here are to make pupils aware of the children they encounter in their lives – at the bus stop, in shops, in the park, in the street playing – and to record what they have seen. At the same time a development study of the young child from birth should be conducted in the classroom, together with data on behaviour, play and children's books. Children up to five years old can be introduced to the classroom with their mothers for observation and guided developmental study. A regular encounter with children and their parents in an in-school playgroup, with the teacher, is most valuable if it can be arranged.

As the pupils' knowledge increases in their recorded observations of children, they should be encouraged to add comment and interpretation arising out of their growing understanding. Initially the pupils should write freely but as knowledge is accumulated the teacher needs to provide a study guide to focus the pupils' observations on particular areas of study which should coincide with the learning programme in the classroom. Topics such as play, reading, television, playground activities and behaviour in the supermarket are all useful topics.

Studying a particular child

This should be undertaken in the second part of the course when the pupils have already observed a variety of children and have explored the relevant experiences in their own childhood, ie things they have been afraid of, what had triggered their naughty deeds, what they had played with and how they had organised their own games. The pupils will need to spend time with the child. They will need to ask parents about pregnancy, birth and first days, always remembering that they may be dealing with sensitive memories. Therefore they *must* be tactful and not press for parents to answer any questions about topics they are reluctant to talk about.

Other areas of study should include play, naughty behaviour, fears, questions children ask, watching television, stories and books read to the child, relationships with parents, siblings, friends, relatives, pets and toys; new experiences should be recorded and the pupil should be responsible for organising outings with the child they are studying – such as a visit to a place of interest, a picnic in the local park. It is also important to experience putting the child to bed.

The concluding part of the study should summarise the developing mental changes that take place during the time of study, eg physical growth, skills acquired, language development, emotional maturation, and so on.

The study should include photographs and drawings made by the child to mark developmental progress. The pupil should be encouraged to write a story for the child, perhaps to prepare him for a new experience or about anything the child is interested in. Stories featuring the child as the main character are always popular. An educational toy could be made to help practise in a new skill the child is acquiring and the pupil can always help with organising a party for the child study group or help out the family by babysitting.

When we recall our own childhood we facilitate our understanding of children; we begin to see things from the child's point of view, ie the child's demands, his responses to situations, his curiosity – his fears, which can seem so baffling, unpredictable and often threatening. But when these are seen from our own childhood's vantage point they become understandable, and our adult response to the child becomes confident. Although each individual is unique there are enough shared experiences to find common ground, and then a positive, constructive communication can be achieved with the child.

Young people moving from childhood to adulthood establish a generation gap – 'You don't understand me – It was different in your day – You are old fashioned – Out of touch' they cry at their parents. A natural metamorphosis, but one which can create scars and which alters the relationship irrevocably. The young adult is unwilling to accept that the adult, be he a parent or a teacher, was also once a confused and defiant teenager. There are too many unresolved conflicts for both sides to forge a link. But to talk together about childhood can form, for each, a new understanding.

Young people need to learn about childhood with an historical perspective. They also need to speculate about the future. Each family, some with grandparents who are still alive, has its own fascinating oral history. Even a relatively simply enquiry such as 'where were you born, Grandma?' or 'Where did you think babies came from?' can trigger a valuable discussion. The modern concepts about birth become much more meaningful when looked at in an historical perspective, particularly when information is derived from first-hand research.

If shared and documented, learning becomes exciting and meaningful.

Arrangement of students' work

A *large file* with different coloured dividers (I use coloured duplicating paper) to separate different sections has proved to work.

A *rough note book* for taking notes, making observations, working in rough, can be clipped to the folder. I feel it is very important to make pupils aware of all the topics which refer to children that are covered in the media.

A *large brown envelope* attached to the folder can house a collection of pictures of children and any magazine articles or newspaper reports about children. These can be used to illustrate work or add information when a particular topic is being studied.

Students should be asked to cover folders with attractive paper and a protective plastic covering. It is also a good idea to encourage them to illustrate work with photographs: photographs of students as children which illustrate family data often ensure that the folder is well looked after and not lost. Photographs displayed on black paper show up to the best advantage.

Suggested folder order
1 Family data
    Emotional development
    Mischief
2 Work on children's books
3 Work on play
4 Naughty behaviour
5 Untruths children tell
6 Preparing children for new experiences
    New baby
    Going to the dentist
    Stay in a hospital
    Starting school
    Going to a party
    Going on holiday, etc
7 Children in special circumstances
8 Work with children
    Playgroup observations and data
    Observations of children in:
        supermarkets
        street play
        at the cinema, etc
    Children's parties
    Babysitting

PART I

Having a Baby

Where I thought babies came from
I used to think that you could have a baby just by
walking up a wedding aisle with a man, then he
would put a ring on your finger, and you would be
pregnant.

How it all begins

Before I begin on the main text, I am going to describe, quite technically, and dispassionately, how a baby is formed, how it grows inside a woman's body and how at the end of the nine months a unique individual is able to sustain an independent life.

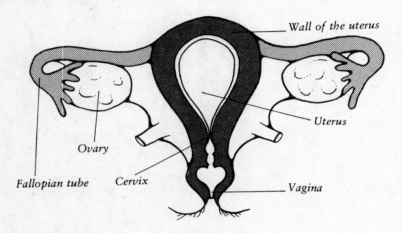

THE FEMALE REPRODUCTIVE SYSTEM; *the wall of the uterus is cut away to show the interior*

Inside the body

Inside a woman there are two little sacs, about the size and shape of walnuts, these are called **ovaries**. They lie below the waist, one on either side. Each ovary contains hundreds of thousands of unripe eggs; these are tiny cells about the size of a full stop. (A baby girl when she is born already has all these eggs inside her ovaries.) Each **ovary** is connected to the **uterus** by narrow tubes called **fallopian tubes** (named after a doctor who first described them). These tubes are about 10cm long and they lead from just beside the ovaries into the uterus.

The **uterus** (womb) is the muscle bag in which the baby grows. It is about the size and shape of a small pear. It has very thick muscular walls which have the remarkable ability to expand as the baby grows inside them.

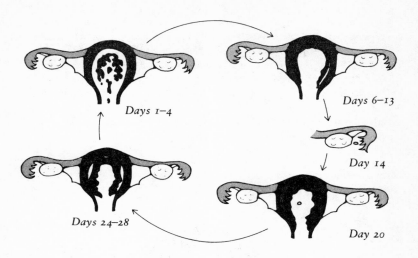

Days 1–4

Days 6–13

Day 14

Day 20

Days 24–28

MENSTRUAL CYCLE:

Days 1–4	During a period the egg, uterus lining and a little blood leaves the body
Days 6–13	The uterus starts to build a fresh lining
Day 14	The egg is released from one or other of the ovaries and begins its journey along the fallopian tube
Day 20	The egg reaches the uterus which is now ready to receive the fertilized egg
Days 24–28	The lining of the uterus reaches maximum thickness
Day 28	The lining of the uterus breaks down and the next period begins

Menstruation – the monthly 'period'

When a girl reaches puberty and becomes a young woman, her body prepares itself for the possibility of becoming a mother, growing a child within her body and giving birth to a new being. Each one of us has a biological time clock. The pituitary gland sends out chemical messages called **hormones** and there is no choice about when this will happen!

Part of this preparation is the growth of her breasts. Other signs are the appearance of hair under her arms and in the pubic area, and her body shape changes.

Each month one egg ripens and is released from one of the ovaries. This is called **ovulation** and usually occurs about 14 days after the beginning of the last period. The ripened egg then begins a long journey through the **fallopian tube** to the **uterus**. The ovaries take turns, each sending one egg to the uterus every other month.

To develop into a baby, it has to meet and join with a sperm cell from the male on the way.

Every month the uterus prepares its chamber for the possibility of **conception**. Much in the same way that birds in spring will feather their nests with the softest moss, so in the uterus the walls build up a coating of blood vessels and mucous to provide a safe nesting place for the fertilized egg.

If the egg is not fertilized (ie does not meet up with a male sperm within 20 hours after it leaves the ovary), the egg and the extra lining built up inside the uterus will fall away through the vagina, and out of the woman's body in a monthly spring-cleaning ritual which lasts from three to five days. This is called **menstruation** – the woman's monthly period.

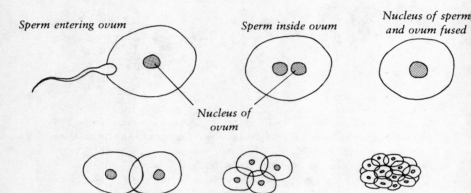

Sperm entering ovum   *Sperm inside ovum*   *Nucleus of sperm and ovum fused*

Nucleus of ovum

THE BEGINNING OF NEW LIFE- *division of fertilized ovum*

Conception
If the egg is fertilized (meets with a male sperm), as it passes through the **fallopian tube** from one of the **ovaries** on the way to the **uterus**, the egg becomes implanted within an inside wall of the uterus.

The woman then misses her period and is pregnant. *Now the body of a new being is growing inside her body.*

Pregnancy
The strange feelings which a woman experiences when she becomes pregnant are caused by her body adjusting to the changes brought about by the developing baby. Her hormones are now preparing her body for pregnancy and child birth.

Hormones
Hormones are chemicals produced by special glands in the body. They circulate in the blood, carrying messages to different parts of the body.

Signs of pregnancy
Every pregnancy is slightly different and it is unlikely that all the signs listed below will be noticed in one pregnancy alone.

Missing a period

Having a very short period with little loss of blood

Changes in the breasts:
    Swelling
    Tingling, throbbing – even hurting
    Veins showing up more clearly
    Nipples and surrounding area darkening

The need to pass water more often

Being constipated

Having an increased vaginal discharge

Feeling, or even being, sick

Changing tastes: going off some foods, eg coffee, alcohol, spicy foods.
    Developing cravings for certain foods

Being more tired and wanting to go to bed much earlier in the evening

The baby

Growing in the uterus

It takes four days for the 'human seed' to be swept along the fallopian tube to the uterus. During this time it has divided and sub-divided to make a solid ball of cells which burrows itself into the spongy lining of the uterus which nature has prepared to receive it. The seed then produces the **placenta** which becomes the life support system for the baby.

1   The placenta provides food
2   The placenta provides oxygen
3   The placenta takes away waste products
4   The placenta acts as a filter for some harmful germs and drugs
5   The placenta produces hormones which regulate the pregnancy and prepare the woman's body for child birth.

The various developments during the nine months of pregnancy are:

One month

By the fourth week the **embryo** is the size of a grain of wheat but this tiny creature has a head, a trunk, arms and leg 'buds'. The heart, which will work for a lifetime, has begun to beat and pushes the blood around the baby's body to and from the **placenta**. The body is enclosed in a transparent waterproof bubble of membrane in which the baby is kept warm and safe from any kind of external shock.

Before two months the baby may be affected by drugs taken by his mother, by virus infections or X-rays.

Two months

Now the baby is called a **foetus**, not an embryo, and it is basically fully formed.

All the parts of a full term baby are present. The foetus is 2.5cm long. Two periods have now been missed by the mother to be, and it is around this time that she will have had her pregnancy confirmed.

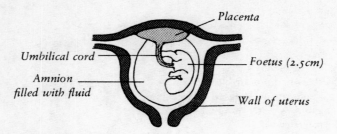

FOETUS AT TWO MONTHS

The foetus is most sensitive to injury in the first eight or so weeks of life, when forming its major internal organs and limbs.

Three months

The **uterus** can now be felt in the lower abdomen as a soft swelling. By twelve weeks the foetus is about 7.5cm long and the developing skeleton and muscles give it more shape. The foetus can kick, turn its head, purse its lips and swallow the **amniotic fluid** (the bag of fluid in which the baby grows). The tooth buds appear now, so calcium from the mother is important. The kidneys are perfected and will pass some urine.

It is possible at this stage to tell from its appearance whether the baby is a boy or a girl. Individual babies now begin to look distinctly different. *A 12-week old baby has all its systems formed. During the remaining six months the baby will begin to practise using them.*

The middle period of pregnancy

No new organs are made, but the ones established in the first three months become more mature.

This is the time when the baby grows very fast in size and weight together with increased activity such as kicking.

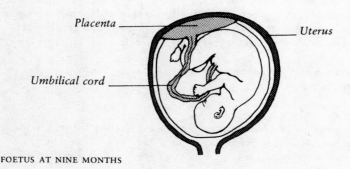

FOETUS AT NINE MONTHS

The final three months

During the last 12 weeks the brain grows rapidly, and protective fat is put on. The baby will practise some of the skills needed after birth and so in these last weeks finger sucking will be a priority.

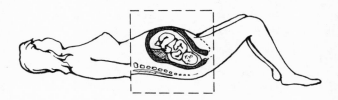

Where the baby has been growing

The baby is inside a bag of water called the **amnion** which is thin, made of layers and filled with amniotic fluid – a good diet helps keep the amnion strong and from breaking too soon.

Amniotic fluid

Often called the *waters*. This is a clear, salty fluid that surrounds the baby inside the amnion and acts as a shock absorber.

From the fourth month, the baby drinks several millilitres of amniotic fluid every day. It is part of the baby's food before birth.

Uterus

A very powerful muscle bag called the *uterus* or *womb* surrounds the amnion. During pregnancy the uterus expands to about 30 times larger than its original size (a small pear). This strong muscle holds and protects the baby.

Cervix

The opening of the uterus is called the *cervix*. It is much thicker than the sides of the uterus during pregnancy and is designed to hold the baby.

Placenta

This is a large 'liver like' organ that is attached to the wall of the uterus. A network of roots spring from it which grow into the wall, very much in the same way as the roots of a tree embed in the soil from which they draw up nourishment for the tree. The baby's blood circulating through the placenta can come very close to the mother's blood circulating in the walls of the uterus, but a membrane separates the two circulations so that the baby's blood and the mother's blood never mix. The *membrane* is thin enough to act as a sieve and lets some substances cross from one blood stream to another. The baby receives food and oxygen from the mother's blood, while waste from the baby's body passes into the mother's blood through the placenta.

The umbilical cord

The *umbilical cord* connects the baby to the placenta. This is a thick twisted cord of blood vessels which enters the baby in the centre of its belly. The umbilical cord is cut after the baby is born. When the small piece attached to the baby falls off, approximately a week after birth, the belly button remains. At the time of birth, the cord is usually the same length as the child. It is still attached when the baby is born and has to be cut. Directly this happens the baby begins an independent existence.

Mucous plug

The opening of the cervix is sealed with a *mucous plug* from the beginning of pregnancy. This protects the baby and prevents any germs from entering the uterus.

A good diet is important

The baby eats only what the mother eats. What a pregnant woman eats every day are the foods that build the baby's body.

During pregnancy, the growing baby takes what he needs from the mother's body, leaving her weak if she is not eating the right foods. As the baby grows, he takes from his mother a good deal of iron and calcium as well as many other nutrients. The doctor will give the mother careful advice about what food she should eat. He will also tell her which extra things she should take, like vitamins, iron and calcium.

What to eat

The mother should eat a well-balanced diet. This should include:

At least $\frac{1}{2}$ litre of milk a day
3 or 4 eggs per week
Lean meat and fish
Liver once or twice a week
Cheese, butter, yogurt
Plenty of fresh fruit and vegetables

Foods which are best avoided

Foods which have chemical additives and preservatives, very fatty food, highly spiced foods and 'pop' drinks.

A good diet in pregnancy will ensure a normal, healthy, strong baby.

How can a mother's smoking affect the baby?

Smoking during pregnancy affects the growth of the developing baby.

Mothers who smoke 20 or more cigarettes a day have babies whose average birth weight is about 0.54kg less than the average for mothers who don't smoke at all.

The 'small for the age' effect is even more important if the baby is born prematurely. It is thought that at least 1500 babies born in Britain die each year because of the effect of their mother's smoking. Heavy smokers are also more likely to have a miscarriage.

Why does it have this effect?
Nicotine causes the blood vessels in the placenta to become narrower, so that less blood, less food and less oxygen reach the baby.

Smoking can harm the baby all through pregnancy, but it is thought to be especially harmful in the last few weeks. This is because the brain cells are growing rapidly at this stage and smoking reduces oxygen supply to them. In extreme cases this causes the baby to be actually starved of oxygen. This does affect the baby's mental development and deprives it of proper nourishment. Not only does smoking cause the thickening of body cells, but nicotine is a potent drug. If you have read health advertisements aimed at pregnant women you will know that when the poisonous gas, carbon monoxide, is inhaled, the baby gasps in the womb with literally every puff that is taken.

Because the placenta is not able to draw out through its roots the full measure of 'goodies' for the baby, its function is impaired, resulting sometimes in premature birth and the liklihood of a small and less healthy baby. If the expectant mother smokes she is therefore putting the baby at risk. No mother would deliberately erect a barrier which would impair the supply of food and stop oxygen getting to her baby, nor would she willingly do anything to withdraw essential nourishment for the baby's growth. Quite the contrary: were she able to observe what was happening, were this hidden screen visible, she would do all in her power, even if it meant putting herself at risk, to tear down this obstruction which was damaging to her baby. Throughout history women have gone to extreme lengths to acquire food for their babies and to protect them from danger. Yet so many women persist in smoking against medical advice because they cannot see what they are causing to happen.

In pregnancy the placenta is the most important organ in the mother's body and its vital life support processes should be allowed to function without the damage that cigarettes can cause.

After the baby is born he may become a passive smoker if either of his parents smoke near him.

Children of heavy smokers have more coughs, colds and bronchitis.

Pregnancy – how it alters your life

Pregnancy is a healthy female experience and should not be treated as an illness.

Although it is only the mother who will have to go to the doctor and visit the clinic for regular checks on the progress of her pregnancy, yet understanding the stages and preparing emotionally for the birth must be an experience shared by both parents. What is important is that both should take an interest in what is happening to the developing baby and they need to become well informed about the course of pregnancy.

It follows that anything we understand well we can enjoy more. On a beautiful evening everyone can get some pleasure from looking at the stars, but the person who can identify the constellations and knows the mythological origins of the names will have a more meaningful experience and be able to appreciate the phenomena more fully. So it is with the wonder of creation in the growth of human life. It is a time to learn and a time for the couple to share their knowledge with each other.

In certain cultures in other countries, anyone who upsets the pregnant woman is regarded with severe displeasure. The husband, the family and friends all go out of their way to make the future mother feel special. They all conspire to boost her morale and help her feel confident and happy. The way a woman feels and thinks of herself during those months of pregnancy will communicate itself to her child and can bear some relation to the way she is going to respond to the baby when it is born, as well as the likelihood of this affecting the child's personality.

To look attractive is important, and pregnancy is not a time for a woman to think 'I am not going to bother how I dress and anyway I need the money to buy things for the baby'. It's far better to buy a second-hand or cheaper carry cot and pram. Instead, she should allow herself a few extra luxuries and the future father should remember to compliment his wife on the way she looks. He should give her perfume, flowers and encourage her to buy new clothes, insist that she has her hair cut well or buy herself a pretty lipstick. He must strengthen the image she has of herself and help her to consider that she is not only a future mother, but an individual as well. She needs to feel confident that her changing shape is not going to make her less attractive to her husband. Neither should she now compare herself unfavourably with her appearance in the time before her pregnancy. This is all a part of ensuring that the mother to be is happy, which is important not only to herself but also to the child.

There are important beauty-care routines that should be observed right from the beginning. One routine is to rub oil on the breasts, stomach and thighs; this will avoid disfiguring stretch marks later and leave the skin supple. Another, of course, is to keep the muscles in trim with suitable exercises and occasionally it is advisable to wear support tights to prevent varicose veins and, most important of all, plenty of rest should be taken.

Diet in pregnancy

The old wives' saying 'you should eat for two' is very much out of favour, but it seems to me to pin-point a very important fact. The foetus makes great demands and these are catered for before the needs of the woman's own body.

The mother's body acts as a reserve from which the foetus can draw up nourishment; there is no tap the mother can turn off and calculate 'so much for the baby and so much for me'.

Recognising this, it is also for herself that the mother needs to alter her diet by drinking more milk, eating liver and remembering to have plenty of fresh fruit and vegetables. Unless she does this, although her baby may be fine when it is born, it could well be at a cost to herself. She may find that her teeth deteriorate, her skin could lose its youthful suppleness and her hair no longer shines.

The foods to be avoided are cakes, chips, bars of chocolate, cans of coke and any other food which just increases the bulk and will only make her fat and sluggish. Also, highly salted foods should be avoided. A woman should eat, during her pregnancy, the kind of food on which she will later bring up her child.

The weight that should be gained during pregnancy is roughly 11kg – allowing a bit more for tall, big-boned women and less for a smaller woman.

Although pregnancy affects the woman's whole system it does not prevent her from continuing with her everyday commitments. She can carry on working until about ten weeks before the baby is due and in some cases longer – although the employer will usually require a letter from a doctor to confirm that this has his consent. She can take exercise – provided it is not violent – go to parties, enjoy a holiday and, of course, continue normal sexual relations with her partner. Some couples are anxious in case sexual activity should harm or damage the baby, but there is no basis for this anxiety because the baby is cushioned in a fluid sac which effectively protects him. Only if a miscarriage is threatened will the doctor advise a couple not to have sexual intercourse.

The closeness which develops between the couple as they prepare for the birth of their child brings with it an increased sense of unity. They feel more loving towards each other. The sharing of new responsibilities gives their lives together a new dimension.

What happens at ante-natal clinics?
The high standard of care before birth is chiefly responsible for the present day safety of child birth.

Ante-natal care can be found in:

Hospitals
Cottage hospitals
Health centres
Doctor's surgery

Usually the doctor makes the arrangements for the mother to have the baby in hospital. She can have all her ante-natal care at the hospital or the family doctor can be in charge of routine care throughout the pregnancy. Occasionally the ante-natal care is shared by the family doctor and the hospital under the shared-care system. Where the visits are divided the mother has a card known as the co-operation card on which all the pregnancy monitoring records are recorded. This acts as the link between the hospital and her doctor.

The first visit to the ante-natal clinic
The first visit to the ante-natal clinic is a very special occasion: it begins the involvement of professional people such as midwives and doctors. People who work in ante-natal clinics *do* understand that it is difficult for a woman to speak

intimately to strangers, to have to answer personal questions, to undergo a medical examination and to be subject to a variety of tests. They do all they can to put the pregnant woman at her ease.

The first visit usually takes places between 10 and 18 weeks after conception. Routine visits are then made at monthly intervals until the 28th week, every fortnight until the 30th week and then once a week until the birth of the baby.

Questions that will be asked

When was the first day of your last period?
The medical staff need to know this to calculate when the baby will be born.

Have there been any previous pregnancies?
Miscarriages or abortion. Any information is treated as strictly confidential.

Other questions will be about age, occupation, housing. There will also be questions about previous illnesses of the mother and her immediate family.

Certain previous illnesses may mean taking special care during pregnancy. This applies particularly in cases where there have been problems with heart, liver or kidneys. Pregnancy will place extra demand on these organs and this could involve danger to both mother and child unless the doctor is forewarned.

Tests
Once the medical history has been completed the following tests will be carried out:

1   A urine specimen will be required to test for diabetes, kidney disease and unsuspected urinary infection.

2   A sample of blood is taken to find out the blood group. Haemoglobin content. (*Haemoglobin* is a substance which gives blood its colour and plays a vital role in transporting the oxygen in the body.)

This test is carried out at every visit. Blood is checked to see if venereal disease is present. It is possible for a woman to have venereal disease without knowing it. If undetected it can cause harm to both mother and baby. Additional tests may be made to check that the blood contains sufficient antibodies to fight the risk of German measles.

3   Blood pressure is taken and the mother to be is weighed and measured.

The doctor's examination
For the doctor's examination it is usual to have to undress completely, put on a gown and lie under a sheet on an examination couch.

The examination is to check general health. The doctor will insert a metal or plastic instrument into the vagina and inspect the cervix, will feel the abdomen from the outside and will insert fingers deeply into the vagina to determine the size and position of the uterus.

A check is made on size and shape of the pelvic walls to make sure that there is enough room for baby to pass through. Then a smear is taken to detect any possible presence of infection which could be transferred to the baby on his journey through the birth canal.

The regular routine checks carried out in ante-natal clinics are aimed at:

A *Seeing the mother is progressing normally*

The prevention of **anemia** in the mother is an important aspect of ante-natal care. By testing her blood, haemoglobin levels are measured. **Haemoglobin** is part of the blood which carries oxygen around the body and its most important ingredient is iron. The baby takes about a third of the mother's iron and therefore she needs to derive more iron from the food she eats. She is given iron tablets to maintain the right balance.

Lack of iron will make the mother feel tired, lethargic and depressed and have the same effect on the baby.

B *Seeing the baby is developing normally*

Major discoveries have dramatically improved the doctors' ability to see how the baby is developing. One of these is **ultrasound** in checking the health of the baby, his age and size. It can also identify the position of the placenta and the presence of twins. This method is simple and painless and it works by using high frequency sound waves which bounce off parts of the body. The echoes are used to build up a picture of the baby.

There is also a technique called **amniocetesis** which takes less than a minute to perform and does not hurt the mother because it is done under local anaesthetic. A fine needle, thinner than the one used to take blood samples, is inserted through the mother's stomach into the sac of water in which the baby floats. A small amount of fluid is withdrawn. The fluid contains, among other things, cells shed from the baby's skin. From studying these cells the doctor can determine various aspects about the baby, including its sex.

This test is made on mothers known to be at risk, through family history or a particular disorder, such as haemophelia. Women who become pregnant after the age of 40 and run the risk of giving birth to a mongol baby (Down's syndrome) are also given this test.

Ante-natal classes

Having, I hope, convinced you that it is a good thing to go into training for labour I will outline the work which is done in ante-natal classes, which of course doesn't just prepare the mother for delivery, but also gives her some guidance as to how to care for the baby when he or she arrives. The trend towards smaller families, together with the fact that it is likely that the young married couple will not be living near parents or any other members of the family, means that women who expect their first child have no experience of babies.

Ante-natal classes aim to give the mother the confidence to deal with the baby after it is born. Most hospital ante-natal classes usually take place in the daytime. Many show films in the evenings to which the fathers are welcome, or have a couples' class at the end of the course. The relaxation is usually taught by a physiotherapist, and the mothercraft by a midwife who may also give descriptions of the course of labour and talk about practices in the hospital such as the availability of pain relief drugs and at which point in the labour they recommend their use. They will also discuss the different possibilities for delivery – the emphasis of course will be on the normal delivery, but the use of forceps will be explained and whether vacuum extractors (a suction cap sometimes used instead of forceps for bringing the baby quickly out of the birth canal) are in common use. There should also be a trip round the hospital where machinery is explained and questions can be asked. I'm sure that if we know and understand about something we are much more able to cope with it when we meet it – it is the fear of the unknown that gives rise to 'emotional nightmares' and causes irrational fears. With this fact in mind I think that knowing about the procedures involved in a Caesarean birth and understanding the implications for mother and baby must be very reassuring.

One other important aspect of these classes is that one meets other women whose faces will be familiar and therefore comforting when they meet again in the strange new world of motherhood in the post-natal wards.

Natural childbirth is a phrase associated with a particular attitude towards delivery. The idea is that much of the pain that is commonly associated with the delivery is caused by a woman's fear and her ignorance. A pioneer in this country of this method is Dick Reed. His theory is that fear leads to pain and that in turn increases the fear. He believes that if this circle can be broken by knowledge and relaxation then the pain is reduced.

Breathing techniques, used along with relaxation during contractions, will help. As a contraction starts a woman settled in her relaxation technique, breathes through her mouth, becoming fully aware of the rate and depth of breathing. The aim is to breathe slowly and not too deeply. As contractions become stronger, breathing should be shallower to compensate for the automatic tendency to breathe faster. An untrained woman may hold her breath or panic breathe. This will tire her to the point of exhaustion. By learning correct breathing she can conserve her strength for the work of pushing the baby out – labour earns its name!

Many women feel that the hospital ante-natal classes are not detailed or thorough enough in their training programmes and choose to attend classes held by the *National Childbirth Trust*. This is an educational charity which provides classes in prepared birth and parenthood. Teachers usually work within a local branch of the Trust and, hopefully, there will also be, within the group, breast feeding counsellors and post-natal support workers who organise a follow-up service. Teachers in these classes have taken the National Childbirth Trust training course and while slightly over half of them have previously trained as midwives or physiotherapists, the others are women who became teachers after using the Trust's methods for the birth of their own children and finding this helpful. Groups of women, or couples, usually follow a course of about eight classes of two hours each, held either in the teacher's own home or perhaps at a local hall. Fees are charged, to those who can afford them, from which the teacher is paid expenses and a small fee. Sometimes a woman can be accompanied in labour by her teacher who can coach her through the technique learned in classes. Often the husband, who has learned the methods with his wife, can be as helpful in guiding, encouraging and reminding her what to do.

Regular practice of the relaxation and breathing techniques taught in antenatal classes can be done when the afternoon rest is taken. These practice sessions often smooth tension and make it easier for the women to have a good refreshing sleep.

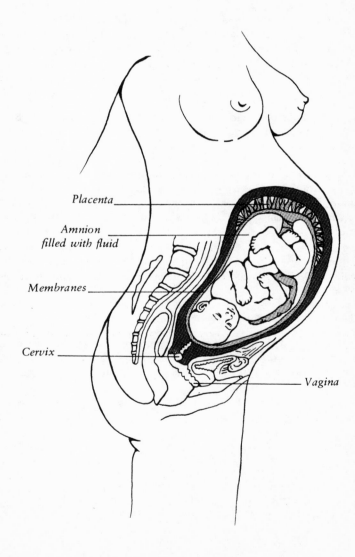

Placenta

Amnion
filled with fluid

Membranes

Cervix

Vagina

Examples from personal experience

Polly and her husband attended classes at the hospital clinic which put her in touch with what the hospital expected to happen during her delivery. She says 'I became familiar with the labour room and made many friends whom I continued to see after our babies were born.

'My husband and I both attended the National Childbirth Trust classes and these I found invaluable. Mine was a long labour but I felt no pain – certainly contractions gave me a strong physical sensation; pushing the baby out was the most physically demanding endeavour I have ever performed, requiring every ounce of my strength and mental concentration. Oh, but I did enjoy it! It seems to me it had in it all the intense anticipation a child feels when waiting for Christmas or for a birthday to arrive – and none of the anti-climax. I found giving birth the most totally joyful and creative time in my life as well as the most hard work.'

The birth

Labour is the process by which the baby leaves the uterus, passes through the neck of the cervix and then the vagina to the outside world. Actual labour begins in one of two ways.

1   *With regular contractions*   The **uterus** tightens, pulling the bag of water in which the baby is lying from the wall of the womb. A small amount of blood mixed with sticky mucous that has been plugging the **cervix** during pregnancy then comes away and is noticed as a 'show' from the vagina.

2   *With the breaking of the waters*   The bag of water usually breaks when the contractions are regular, but it may break much earlier as a first sign of labour.

Labour is divided into three stages

1   *The first stage*   The purpose of contractions in the first stage of labour is to *dilate the cervix*, ie to pull it open so that the baby can emerge. This is the longest stage and can last for 12 hours or for only two or three hours.

Gradually the contractions become stronger and closer together as the cervix opens faster.

2   *The second stage*   The baby is born as soon as the cervix is fully open (10cm). The woman can then push out her baby through the birth canal.

This pushing is not at all painful for most women. It is the more active stage of labour and seldom lasts longer than an hour.

Most babies emerge head first. Some like to be different and arrive bottom first and the delivery is then called a **breech**. Within seconds of the

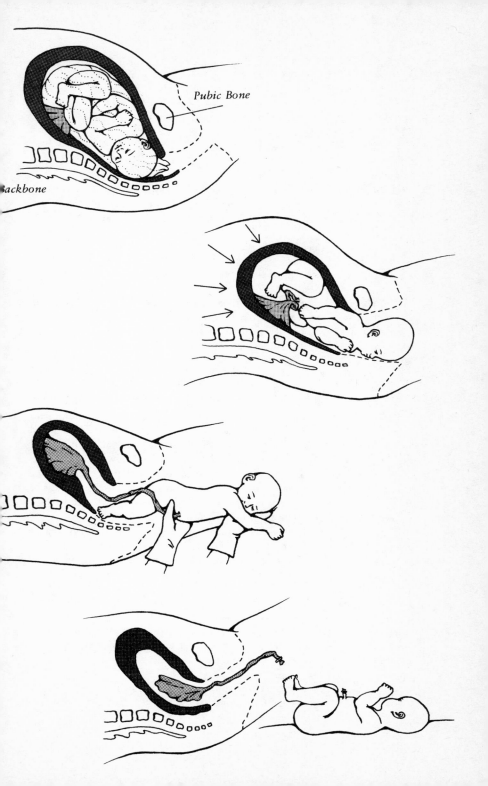

Pubic Bone

Backbone

birth, the baby cries and moves. The cord is then dampened and cut. At this point the baby should be held close to the mother and can be put to the breast to suckle.

3   *The third stage*   At this stage the woman pushes out the afterbirth – the *placenta*, **umbilical cord** and the *amnion*.

The birth sequence is now accomplished.

Pain relief

As a society we no longer accept physical pain. Since the development and general use of pain-relief drugs, for anything from headaches to toe-aches, our level of tolerance towards pain and our familiarity and acceptance of it is very low.

When a woman needs pain relief in labour three methods are available:

1   Inhaling gas
2   Pain-killing injections, such as pethedine
3   An epidural anaesthetic.

Gas inhalation is not effective for long periods but can be very effective at the end of the first stage and, if required, for the second stage and delivery – this has for many years been a popular method. Its advantage is that the mother herself can apply it and have control on just how much she takes, and can reach for it when she needs it. At some time during her ante-natal clinic visits the mother will be shown how to use this aparatus. What she will be inhaling is a mixture of nitrous oxide and oxygen.

Sedatives and tranquillisers can sometimes be given to help a mother relax and sleep, and may be given in the early stages of labour. **Analgesics** – pain killers – are used later – the most frequently used one is pethedine. This is given by injection at intervals of no less than four hours. It works on the brain and makes one feel sleepy and out of touch with reality. The midwife is allowed to administer it. She tries to judge when to give the dose so that its effects will be nearly gone when it is time for the mother to push – otherwise she may not be fully alert to what is happening and not able to co-operate adequately – consequently forceps delivery is more likely.

The method which has been most recently developed is **epidural analgesia**. In this, pain-killing drugs are injected into the lower part of the back, into an **epidural space** which surrounds the spinal cord, for which the nerve supply for the birth area arises. The advantage, of course, is that the method leaves the mother's brain completely clear, unlike the other methods, and very effectively removes all pain and discomfort. The disadvantage is that the mother must hand over to the doctors and midwives all control of her labour and be completely directed by them so, as she is out of touch with what is happening to her body, forceps are almost always used. After such a birth women have often expressed regret that they had felt so little – somehow they have felt cheated of their birth experience.

The epidural method is available only in relatively few maternity units. It can only be given by a doctor specially trained to administer the drug as it requires a high level of skill to do so. Consequently, it is very expensive compared to the other methods available.

General anaesthesia is the traditional method used for a **Caesarian section**. The woman not only loses the pain sensation, but becomes unconscious. The procedure and recovery is the same as happens in all operations when general anaesthesia is used.

The snag with all the pain-relief methods used in childbirth is that whatever drugs are given to the mother do cross the placenta to the baby and it takes time for the effect to wear off. The baby is less alert and can be floppy and disinterested in sucking for a few days after the birth. However, much care is taken to ensure that the right drugs are chosen and the quantity is carefully controlled.

For some women childbirth can be agonisingly painful, but for others that is not their experience. To determine this before the onset of labour is not possible. Undoubtedly a woman who is relaxed in familiar surroundings, with caring people about her will be most able to master her own resources to meet any pain or discomfort and cope with it with no aid from drugs – or just use the minimum amount. However, many women do not give birth in these ideal circumstances and, although hospital delivery has many advantages, such as greater physical safety for mother and baby when complications happen quickly and unpredictably, hospital is for most women a strange and frightening place – associated with illness and pain. The doctor is a formidable person by nature of his status – kind he may be – but most women feel inferior or inadequate in his presence and that is no way to feel when giving birth. Often they relinquish the right to express their own needs and feelings in front of such professional expertise. The midwife, to their grandmother, would have been a familiar person – people after all did not move from area to area as they do now – and she remained local for a period of years. Her hospital counterpart of today is a stranger and for communication between strangers to take place takes time.

The technological appearance of a modern delivery room with its machine, dial monitors and so forth, all conspire to make the mother to be feel that the part she plays in the drama can no way compete. I was taken aback when interviewing grandmothers about the way it was for them to have a baby, to find their memory of the event clear, and their account full of happy reminiscences and anecdotes. They all remembered exactly what they had to get ready, who was there and what it was like. In words of one of them: 'It is nice to have babies!' It was not the same talking to their far more privileged grand-daughters. Many of them cried at some point in their account – not from the memory of the pain – pain relief had been ample – but to them the experience had been overshadowed by a feeling of frustration and inadequacy. 'I couldn't wait to get out of that hospital – I'm not going there again; I made my husband have a vasectomy.' How could this possibly be? The hospitals they attended in most cases were modern, with facilities superior often to their home conditions. It was being among strangers, having a feeling that they were being passed over, treated with patronage. The one thing they all agreed about was how pleased they had been to have their husbands there. 'I couldn't have gone through it without him – he was there all for me – he was the only one I could tell how I felt – he made me try harder when I thought I couldn't make any more effort.' Throughout history, and in all cultures, women have been attended by their female relatives and friends during their all important event. The relaxation of hospital rules allow a women to have her husband or someone of her own during labour is, I feel, an important innovation in giving effective relief from pain in labour.

What have I learned?   Questions on pregnancy

1   Why is it important for the pregnant woman to feel happy and confident?
2   Why should the pregnant woman rub oil on her skin, take exercise, possibly wear support tights and have plenty of rest?
3   If the mother does not alter her diet as suggested, what is likely to happen to her?
4   What weight increase would be expected during pregnancy?
5   How long before the baby is due can a woman continue working if she wishes?
6   What other activities are mentioned which a pregnant woman can continue?
7   What prevents sexual intercourse harming the baby?
8   In what event would a doctor advise a pregnant woman not to have intercourse?
9   When does the first visit to an ante-natal clinic take place?
10   Why are questions asked about heart, liver and kidneys and why is a urine specimen taken?
11   What does haemoglobin do?
12   Why is blood checked to see whether venereal disease is present?
13   Why should the doctor be interested in German measles?
14   Why does the doctor have to insert fingers deeply into the vagina?
15   Why is the shape and size of the pelvic walls checked?
16   Why is a smear taken?
17   If the mother lacks iron, what happens?
18   In your own words tell another member of the class what the following two words mean and when used: ultrasound: amniocetesis.
19   Say in your own words what the value of attending an ante-natal clinic is. What does the author mean by reassuring?
20   What are the advantages of the Natural Childbirth method? Do you think there could be disadvantages?
21   Why should it be necessary for a pregnant woman to learn breathing?
22   Explain what happens in the two different ways labour starts: regular contractions and breaking of the waters.
23   What is the purpose of the first stage of labour?
24   What is a breech delivery?

34

25 Say what happens when epidural analgesia is used to relieve pain in childbirth. What are the advantages and disadvantages?

26 The author contrasts the attitudes of present-day mothers who mainly have their babies in hospitals with that of their grandmothers. What differences did she find? Why do you think this is? This would be a good question to answer through small group discussion.

27 The author is sympathetic to natural childbirth. Why do you think this is? Do you feel the same?

What have I learned?   Questions on having a baby

1   Be certain that you understand meanings of the following words – making notes if necessary:

Ovaries, uterus, fallopian tubes, ovulation, hormones, egg (as used in this chapter), sperm, conception, menstruation.

When you are sure you understand, you and someone else in the class can test each other, or the teacher may give you a test.

2   Now do the same for the signs of pregnancy. Learn them and test each other. By the way – does a woman notice all these signs on becoming pregnant?

3   What happens while the fertilized egg (referred to in the text as 'human seed') travels along the fallopian tube for four days?

4   And what does it first produce when it arrives at the uterus?

5   Learn the five things that the placenta does for the growing baby.

6   The heart starts to beat within the first month. Can you work out from the text why it is needed so soon?

7   You are told of three things the mother must be careful about during the first two months as they are dangerous. Name them.

8   What is the difference between a foetus and an embryo and at what stage does the embryo become a foetus?

9   Why is it important that the mother can give the foetus calcium during the third month?

10   The book says 'a twelve-week-old baby has all its systems formed'. What happens during the other six months of pregnancy?

11   Why do you think the brain grows last of all?

12   Why is it necessary for the unborn baby to practise finger sucking?

13   Make sure you understand the following words and test each other. Amnion, amniotic fluid, uterus, cervix, placenta, umbilical cord, mucous plug.

14   What happens to the mother if she does not eat properly during the pregnancy?

15   What extra things must the mother eat during pregnancy?

16   Learn by heart the foods which are recommended as essential for a pregnant woman and those she should avoid. Test each other.

17   List all the possible harmful effects of smoking.

18   What effect does smoking have on the placenta and therefore the unborn child?

19   What does the book mean when it says the child may become a *passive* smoker if either of his parents smokes near him?

The Myth

Having a baby has always been a very special time – a time that has been surrounded by ritual and myth, prayer and taboo. One very common early belief was that childbirth could be made easier by opening all doors, leaving all locks unlocked and all caged birds freed. The women in the household had to loosen their hair, untie any knots and unbutton any buttons. Other similar rituals were performed symbolic of freeing the baby from the womb. On the other hand anything that was symbolic of constraint was taboo, particularly when birth was imminent. For instance, women who sat near a pregnant woman with their fingers interlaced were accused of sorcery. In Greek mythology there is a tale which illustrates this: the Greek goddess of childbirth was bribed by Juno to sit with her right knee over her left and her hands clasped, in front of Alcmena's door when she went into labour and, in this manner, delayed the birth of Hercules. In India it is the custom for a grain jar to be burst open so that the child will be quickly and easily born.

Couvade is the name given to a curious custom practised in antiquity but still observed today in Indonesia, Burma and parts of South America. This involves the man taking to his bed when his wife is in labour and acting out what she is experiencing. In some parts of Brazil, an Indian woman rises immediately after childbirth while the father goes to bed with the new born baby, receiving the congratulations of friends and relatives. The mother is ignored. The reason for this seems to be that because conception is seen to be entirely dependent upon the male, the woman's role is regarded as passive, rather like a hen hatching an egg. Therefore, once the baby is born the mother's function is seen to be over and it is the father who assumes the close relationship to the newborn child.

In the Bible (*Song of Solomon*, ch. 8, v. 5) there is a reference to the custom of delivering the baby in the open air: '*I raised thee up under the apple tree. There thy mother brought thee forth*'. Open-air deliveries are still common practice among the present-day Bedouin. In certain parts of India and Africa, mothers give birth in a special birth hut into which no-one may enter unless they are directly involved in attending the mother. Both these customs have the useful effect of isolating the mother and baby from possible infection.

In ancient Egypt references were made to birth-stools and these were used in Europe until the eighteenth century. In the Middle East they are still being used today. Women in childbirth crouch on a birth-stool, their bodies in an upright position. One of the women in attendance then sits behind the woman in labour and holds her around the body, while another kneels in front of the woman, ready to take the baby. Bricks are used in some parts of the world instead of birth-stools. It is customary for the woman to sit on her haunches, her knees resting on the clay bricks and her feet on the ground, while her bottom rests on her heels. A midwife then supports her body and another waits for the baby.

Louis XIV used to hide behind a curtain and watch his mistresses giving birth. So that he could have a good view the women were delivered on a flat table. This chauvanistic vicariousness underlines the fact that only in Western Society are women expected to lie flat when giving birth. In most peasant and primitive societies women have always preferred the more normal crouching position. In West Africa today a woman may kneel – or she may even hang from the rafters of her hut swinging backwards and forwards for part of her labour.

In the past, women in labour have always been attended by other women. Helping with labour was a skill women were expected to acquire in the same way as they were expected to learn to cook. In Elizabethan times, for instance, when a woman went into labour in England it was a signal for all her friends to join together for a party. Alcohol was drunk by everybody, including the mother, and a good time was had by all.

Fifty years ago, in most working-class English homes, birth was still very much part of a ritual. The nurse was paid a couple of pounds to attend the birth and she would come daily for 14 days after the birth. Although there was much ignorance as to what exactly happened when the baby was born, women were brought up on no-nonsense statements like 'what went in would have to come out'. The nurse was local and known by everyone in the community.

First of all the bed was prepared for the lying-in: usually it was padded with newspaper and sheets of brown paper. A jug and basin, a chamber pot, two towels and two bowls – one to wash the mother and one to wash the baby – were prepared. Then there was a disinfectant for the nurse to scrub her hands in, a paste jar for the thermometer plus cotton wool and towels. A reel of white thread was provided to tie the umbilical cord. Thick cotton twill was used to bind the mother's stomach for 14 days after the birth, and a small strip was sewn round the baby's middle to retain the belly button. The twill was also tied to the bottom of the bed for the mother to pull on when she was pushing. Nappies were made from a towelling roll.

When born, the baby was held upside down and had his bottom slapped. The after-birth was taken downstairs and handed to the father for him to burn in the grate. The number of 'pops' it made were supposed to indicate how many children the couple would have.

Then the bottom drawer of the chest was made into a bed for the baby and this rested on two chairs next to the mother's bed. After the birth the mother would have to stay in bed for 14 days and she would not even be allowed to place her feet on the floor. It was also customary for the mother of the newly delivered woman to sleep in the same bed as her daughter for the 14 days – and for the husband to sleep on his own.

Charms, amulets and talismans have been used throughout the world at the time of birth. Women have also clutched 'a virgin nut'. These nuts were kidney-shaped, marked with a cross and were sometimes found washed up on beaches.

Any midwife who had a 'virgin nut' in the Middle Ages would be in great demand, for these nuts were meant to help the woman have a safe and speedy delivery. Red thread and bunches of rowan berries would decorate the walls of the labour room for these were supposed to keep away the evil eye, and a tiny trinket, given as a love token, would be hidden in the pregnant's woman's clothing, pinned to the right thigh so that the fairies would not steal the baby or the breast milk.

All that was a long time ago. Recently in a very modern hospital a mother whose daughter had just gone into labour rushed into the sister's room and thrust some money into her hand – 'For research' she said. What instinct made her do that? Who did she want to appease? Had she hoped the 'ritual appeasement' would bring her daughter safely through labour?

Nowadays most women are expected to have their babies in hospital and it takes a determined effort on the part of any woman to arrange to have her baby in her own home. Doctors often find it difficult to understand why a woman does not want to have her baby in hospital, particularly when they carefully explain the greater risks that a woman exposes herself and her baby to if she has her baby at home.

What have I learned   Questions on the myth

1   What are the meanings of the words 'ritual', 'myth', 'taboo'?

2   What was the purpose of the rituals mentioned in the first paragraph of this chapter?

3   Explain *why* certain things mentioned in the first paragraph were considered taboo.

4   What advantage is there to the birth ritual mentioned as occurring in parts of India and Africa?

5   Describe in about 150 of your own words the ritual of working-class English births.

6   What was the purpose of the talismen mentioned as used in the Middle Ages?

7   Discuss with a friend or in a small group any rituals, taboos or myths about childbirth that you have heard of or come across that are used today.

8   Why do you think people need these things?

Introduction to
Family Data Work Guide

Having acquired a body of knowledge about menstruation, conception, pregnancy, birth and the newborn baby, it is time to use another component of the course: getting in touch with your own childhood to widen the field of study.

The questionnaire entitled *Family Data* and *Emotional Development* when completed will produce research data which can be used in a variety of ways.

Read a recorded example of such a data and the findings made by the class from it about children. Compare it to your own and that of your class. See how far back in your family you can research. Your discoveries will give a very interesting 'historical dimension' to your work. If possible illustrate your work with photographs.

EXAMPLE

KNOWLEDGE LEARNED FROM FAMILY DATA FILES

Introduction
Important facts were taken from everybody's files and were put together to form this essay:

Birth
Nearly all of our grandparents were born at home. There would have been a local midwife who was known by all the women who just accepted that this woman was going to deliver their child. One such midwife would have quite a large district to cover. She would carry on working until she was, usually, between 65 and 75. The midwife literally lived off the families whom she dealt with – they would give her food and money for her help. The families were very much larger than they are today – my Nan was the youngest of 19 children. My great grandmother didn't have much time on her hands to look after my Nan. My Nan was forever crying so her mother gave her a 'sugar dummy' made from bread which had been soaked in a sugar solution wrapped into a small piece of muslin cloth. This was said to be able to 'keep my Nan quiet for hours'. When the time comes I will not have any choice where I have my children – they will have to be born in hospital.

Milestones

Some of us never crawled – but just began to walk at around the age of 13 months. Some also wriggled about a lot on their bottoms instead of crawling. The child's first smile is very important because it is a large step between the bonding of mother and child. The child is responding to all the love and care which he has been given. His way of repayment is this big beaming smile which most parents can't wait to see.

Dreams

People's dreams were all very similar. One person had a dream about running along a highway chased by a large truck. Another dreamt about flying downstairs and many dreamt about losing their mums whilst out shopping. In all of these cases they woke up before something terrible happened like being run over, or hitting the bottom of the stairs.

Comforters

Most of us had a comforter of some kind. They range between a Golly and a pair of red wellingtons all of which one of us couldn't sleep without. If a comforter managed somehow to get lost the child wouldn't be at all happy until it was found. When I was small I had a little doll called Tina. One summer's day we went up country to my uncle's house. In the evening we went to a small country pub which had a beer garden. I took Tina with me. Unfortunately I fell asleep before leaving the pub and Tina was left on a bench. I noticed the next morning when I woke up – and was very upset. We telephoned my uncle and he said that he would try to get her back and bring her down to me the following day. He did – it seems very silly now but I was so happy to see my doll.

Many children suck their thumbs or have a dummy as a comforter. This usually stops when the child is about five – when he begins school. If he is still sucking his thumb he is told what a baby he is and that the other children will laugh at him. This usually frightens the children into stopping.

Bedtime

Bedtime just has to be one of the happiest parts of our family data. Bedtime has to be planned very carefully by the parents. It can be a very insecure time for the child because it is being parted from its parents. Bedtime, for a child, distinguishes night from day. If the child looks forward to bedtime then he won't be afraid of night – but if he hates bedtime he will probably be afraid during the night. Bedtime should last at least half an hour. During which time you should read him a story, play with him and of course love and cuddle him. A child will not enjoy bedtime if it is too abrupt, maybe both parents are not there or if his parents don't seem to be enjoying it. If a child will not go to bed don't give in to him but then again don't just smack him and pack him off to bed. A child should never be frightened into going to bed by someone saying something like 'If you don't go to bed now the monster will get you' or, at Christmas, 'If you are a naughty girl Santa won't leave any presents'. Comments like these will make the child frightened about going to bed so you're no nearer to solving your problem.

Most children enjoy having a story before going to sleep. Most of us had fairytales told to us but they were not read straight from the book but were translated into simple language so that we could understand it. Many of our parents used puppets and dolls to animate the story. Children also like stories which are about themselves.

It is very important for children to hear people talking even if they are telling stories. They need to hear the words and watch how the words are being formed. Bedtime can be fun for both the child and the parents if you care enough to bother.

Jealousy

When Caroline's younger sister was born she had dislocated hips and had to have both of her legs in plaster – therefore had to be carried everywhere. Being just a small child Caroline didn't realise that her sister was ill – she thought that her sister was being favoured. Caroline became very jealous of her sister and began to make up excuses like her legs ached so that she would be carried too.

When children are ill they regress – or go back to an earlier stage. They become unindependent and want their mothers and a lot of affection. Even now when I'm ill or worried about something I find myself wanting my Mum – I think that it's just nice to know that somebody cares.

Funny stories

Between us all we have some very funny stories:

Linzi was about three years old when she was asked to be bridesmaid at her sister's wedding. During the service Linzi stood up and shouted at the top of her voice 'I've got frilly knickers on'. Was Linzi being naughty and rude? No she wasn't. Linzi was very proud of her frilly knickers and thought that everybody might like to know.

Another one of us went out one day on the bus with her Mum. Whilst travelling a black woman got on. The small girl had never seen a black person before and wondered if the woman had dipped her face into chocolate pudding.

Both of the comments of these stories were said very innocently. Maybe if the girl in the second story had not asked about the chocolate pudding she would have thought wrongly about black people for a great deal longer. This is all part of understanding *life*!

Whilst talking to my Mum she managed to recall many other funny stories about me – like the time we went to London Zoo for the day. Suddenly my Mum and Dad realised that I was missing. They hunted for me for half an hour – and were at their wits' end. They eventually spotted me in what seemed to be a large glass building – it was the reptile house. My Mum and Dad walked round it trying to find a way in. There was a small door at the back and my Mum had to find a keeper to get me out because the public were not supposed to go in.

Another time my Mum and I went shopping. At the pay out my Mum put a yogurt onto the conveyor belt so as to pay for it. I picked it up and began shaking it. The foil split and the Strawberry yogurt went everywhere over the till, over my Mum, over our trolly and even over the cashier – but funnily enough it missed me.

On another shopping trip we were returning home when my Mum noticed a man's shoe under my pram blanket. It was brand new and my Mum presumed that I'd taken it from a shop's outside display – that I had. We walked back along the street and I showed my Mum the shop and we went in. She handed the assistant the shoe and apologised for me having taken it. He burst out laughing and said not to worry because it was the second time that it had happened that day. He thanked Mum for being so honest and returning the shoe. Then he began laughing again and asked my Mum what I was planning to do with it. My Mum smiled sweetly and we left.

Emotional traumas

Emotional traumas can occur in many different circumstances. A sudden change of scene like going into hospital could cause one. A child needs to be prepared for a situation like this.

It is frightening enough for an adult to have to go into hospital. So what must it be like for a small child.

I last went into hospital when I was eleven. One evening I was watching television when I felt a severe pain in my stomach. My Mum phoned the doctor and he came. He examined me and found me to have appendicitis. The doctor phoned an ambulance and I was taken to the Royal Alex. It all happened so quickly that I didn't have time to feel frightened – and anyway I was in so much pain that I didn't care what they did to me as long as they made me well again. It was only when I recovered and realised where I was that I began to worry.

It must be terrible for a young child going into hospital not knowing what's going to happen to them. The fact that the child will have to go into hospital for an operation should be introduced slowly over a large period of time so that the child is used to the idea and begins to accept it.

Knowledge and wisdom

We have learnt a lot from our family datas but some points are more relevant and important than others:

Mothers and fathers should treat problems in exactly the same way – the child may get away with being naughty by one parent and be smacked by another. The child should not have the ability to play one parent against the other.

Children learn by example. If the child sees you smoking then he will probably imitate you. I don't think that smoking and drinking should be eliminated from the child's life though because I think that the child grows up wishing that he was allowed to do it. The boy or girl will probably begin smoking behind his or her parents' backs.

When I was about five years old my Mum and Dad never stopped me from having a small sip of their sherry or a puff of my Dad's cigarette. Now neither the thought or fascination of smoking or drinking appeals to me – but when my friend was smaller her parents kept drink and smoking well away from her – now whenever we go to a party of something she drinks a lot behind her parents back just to try and get back at them.

Children's fears and dislikes should be taken into consideration. If a child comes downstairs saying that there's a tiger under the bed then don't tell her off and send her back to bed because it won't make things any better as children's fantasies are very near to reality – it is much better for you to tell the child that you are going up to shoot it or capture it – this way the child will believe that it has really gone.

Many children don't like walking over the grids in pavements. They don't understand about volume and think that they will fall down it. The way to overcome this is not by forcing the child into walking over it but by trying to explain how it works and by walking over it yourself.

EXAMPLE

FAMILY DATA FILE (JAYNE)

Place and date of birth

I was born in Brighton on 4 October 1966. My Mum was born in Brighton too on 27 October 1944. My Nan was born on 22 October 1907 in Great Hookham, Norfolk.

Birth

My birth took 48 hours, my Mum's took eight hours and my Nan couldn't remember. No forceps were used in any case.

My Nan was delivered by the woman next door as the nearest doctor was more than five miles away. When my Nan was carrying my Mum she didn't have a clue where the baby was going to be born from – and only really found out when told by an older sister that 'what goes up must come down'. Before hearing that she thought that the baby burst out of her stomach when it was due to be born.

Graph showing family ages

```
90
80
70
60
50
40
30
20
10
 0
```

| Grandad | Nan | Dad | Mum | Jayne | Geraldine |

Illness and Inoculations

When I was a small child I had chicken pox, German measles and mumps.
I can remember having both chicken pox and mumps. I had chicken pox
first. It was during the winter so I had to be well wrapped up in blankets
and dressing gowns which made me very hot, and irritated my spots
something awful. The doctor told my Mum to keep me very warm, and
that was what she intended to do. I had to sit in the living-room with the
gas fire on full blast, all day. I have calomine lotion dabbed on my spots
about twice an hour. This did stop the itching for about five minutes but it
soon came back again. Mumps came next. One morning I woke up with a
very sore throat, it was so dry that even having a drink didn't make it any
better. By the end of the day the right-hand side of my throat had swollen
to at least twice its normal size. This was very uncomfortable and I cried a
lot with it. I was given medicine for it but it didn't seem to do any good —
and it tasted awful.

Food

My Nan, my Mum and I were all breast-fed for nine months. I never had
powdered milk but my sister did because my Mum couldn't breast-feed
her for very long. I first began to eat solid foods when I was six months old.
I had the same as the rest of the family but puréed. My Mum ate solids
when she was seven months and my Nan when she was 12 months.

Milestones

I first smiled when I was eight weeks old. My Mum was playing with me
and I gave a little smile. This pleased her very much because both her and
my Dad had been looking forward to it. My Nan thought that my Mum
first smiled when she was two weeks old — but a sister said that it was
'wind'. She first really smiled at eight weeks. I first talked when I was 10
months old and my Mum first spoke when she was 12 months. We both
said dadadadadada. . . .

Emotional development

When I was a small child I think that I most cared about my Mum and Dad. I know that it is not always your parents who come first but in my case I think it was. My Mum was with me all day and in the evening when Dad arrived home from work he had his tea and then took me off Mum's hands.

Bedtime was very good fun for me because it involved the whole family. First of all Mum would undress me and tuck me up in bed then Dad would gather all of 63 stuffed toys including a big dog called Mungo and a large Womble made by my Mum. He would put them down on the floor by him and one by one would pick them up and kiss them goodnight, then let them kiss me goodnight before placing them at the end of my bed. Mungo and the Womble could not come on my bed because they were too big and there was no room for me. After the commotion with the toys Mum would read me my favourite story which was the fairytale *Cinderella*. Mum knew the story and would not read straight from the book, she would use it as a guideline and then *ad lib* so as to make it more understandable for me.

I had a room to myself until my sister was born then we had to share. When Geraldine was too big to sleep in a cot we shared a double bed for eight months because we were moving and it wasn't worth buying new beds until we had moved into our new home. We had good fun during those eight months jumping up and down on our beds when we should have been asleep and quickly getting into bed when we heard either Mum of Dad coming. Sometimes we got caught but luckily Mum and Dad took it in good heart. When we moved into our new flat Geraldine and I still had to share a room and Mum and Dad brought us bunk beds. You wouldn't believe what good fire-engines those beds made.

When I was very small I used to hate men. When one of my uncles for example walked into the room I would scream and shout and rush to find my Mum. I had hysterics when a man tried to pick me up. Nobody knows why I was like this. It can't have been because I wasn't used to men because I was always with my Dad and Grandads. My Mum thought that it was because I wasn't with my uncles very often – but I took very well to my aunties.

I never had a dummy, a bottle and neither did I suck my thumb. When my Nan was a baby she had sugared bread, which was bread soaked in a syrup solution, put in a muslin cloth instead of a dummy. My Nan was the youngest of 19 children and her mother had such a lot of work to do and she didn't have a lot of time to look after my Nan so she gave her the sugared bread as a comforter to stop her crying instead of a dummy.

I began to be potty-trained when I was only two months old. My Mum put the potty on her lap and then sat me on top of it. Once when getting ready to return home from Devon after a holiday Mum and Dad had packed both of our cases but had not shut them so as not to screw and crease the clothes up. I decided to do toilet on the top of my Mum's case.

45

I'm not quite sure why I did it but I knew it was wrong so I tried to keep out of Mum's and Dad's way for the rest of the day. When the time came for the shutting of the suitcase I felt a bit worried. They were astonished by what they saw – and Dad asked me if 'it was mine'. Luckily for me they saw the funny side of it – but they still tease me about it today.

Since when I was about four years old I've had a craze for cheese which I have never grown out of. Then when I was about seven I began another craze for macaroni and pasta – that led to my love for macaroni cheese. When I began to eat solid foods my two favourites were boiled egg with 'soldiers' and toast and Marmite. I still love hot toast and Marmite.

When I was seven I had an accident at school in which I cut my head open. An ambulance was called and I was taken to the Alex. I was given an injection by a Chinese nurse which put me to sleep so that I could have my face stitched. Whilst asleep I had a horrible dream in which there was a continuous picture of my Mum, with a very white, worried face wearing bright red lipstick, surrounded by about seven pictures of the Chinese nurse. This, I know, was caused because I was under the anaesthetic but I get that same dream even now. When I see women wearing bright lipstick it brings it back to me.

The only thing I was afraid of, apart from men, was Santa Claus. But then again I don't think that it was a fright, more of an excitement. On Christmas Eve we left mince-pies, sherry, orange squash and two bowls of water for Santa and his reindeer. I would never have dared to peep, let alone get up to go to the toilet or get a drink in case 'he' saw me and told me off and didn't leave me any presents. It's funny that both of my fears were men. I wasn't at all worried about going to see Santa in Hanningtons. Every year my Mum, my sister and I used to meet my Nan at the bottom of St James's street for our annual visit to 'Santa's Grotto'. After going into a lift and either going down in a submarine or up in a space rocket we would walk through one of the many fairytale lands before receiving our present from Santa. Afterwards Nan would treat us to a cup of tea and a slice of cream cake in Fortes.

I can remember one winter's day when I was very small, it had been snowing the previous night and my Dad decided to take me for a walk along to the 'Level' children's playground. There is a small pond in the Level which had frozen over. I decided to do some ice skating – but the ice wasn't hard enough and my feet went straight through. The water flooded over the top and down into my little red wellingtons. My dad pulled me out and we had to be on our way home. My little red wellies squeaked all the way home.

When I was young I knew that babies grew inside the mother's stomach but I didn't know how they got there in the first place. I knew this because my Mum was carrying my sister Geraldine when I was three years old. My Mum explained to me that I was going to have a little brother or sister. I was able to feel Geraldine kicking inside by putting my hand onto my Mum's stomach.

I was due to start school at Carton Hill infant school in the January so the October before my Mum and I went in to the school for a look around and a chat with the teachers. I was to have a teacher called Miss Dyer so Mum and I went to see her. I began to play a game with a girl in the class while Mum talked to the teacher. Before long I felt one of the class and I was sorry when we had to leave. I was very excited about starting school. When the big day came, Mum took me to school and left me with the other children in the playground. There were a lot of tears from some of the children — but not one from me. I was happy to be starting school. This I think is because my very first experience of school was a happy one.

FAMILY DATA WORK GUIDE

Birth
Where were you born — your mother — your grandmother?
How long did the birth take — were forceps used?

Family
Make a graph showing ages of the members of your family.

Illnesses
Which childhood infections, diseases did the members of your family have?
Which have you had?
Which inoculations did you have?
Did your mother and grandmother have the same?

Food
When you were born were you breast-fed — if so for how long?
Were you given powdered milk — which brand?
When did you have solids — cereal?
When did you start eating the same food as the rest of your family?

Milestones
How old were you when you first smiled — sat up — crawled — walked?
What was your first word?
How old were you when you started to talk?

If you cannot find this information about yourself 'adopt' a small child and get this data from the mother.

You will be able to introduce further data. This is only a guide from which you can branch out.

Emotional development
Who were the people you most cared about?
Who did you fear or dislike — for what reason?

Did you suck your thumb – have a dummy – when did you stop?
Was there a toy or a blanket you always took to bed?
Can you remember what form your bedtime took?
Did you have a story read – do you remember a favourite one?
Did you share your room with brothers or sisters?
When were you potty-trained?
Can you remember anything about it?
Did you have any food fads?
Do you still have them?
Do you recall any dreams and nightmares you had?
List the things you were afraid of.
Do you know any funny stories about yourself?
Where did you think babies came from?
Write in detail about your first memories.

Introduction to Playgroup sessions

In the Introduction I made suggestions how a classroom can easily be turned into a playgroup for several children accompanied by their mothers. A *Playgroup Task Sheet* provides a guide to how students can most profitably spend their time during such a session. As the work progresses, playgroup sessions can focus on a particular topic. I include a guide to one on behaviour which can be used at the same time as the concentrated work on behaviour is done in Part III of the book. The same kind of focus can be placed on other topics; such as play, children's reading, or safety, during playgroup sessions – or can be applied if only one or two mothers and children are invited to the classroom.

Playgroup task sheets

Instructions
Make parents and children feel welcome: introduce yourself. Offer to carry bags, pushchair, etc.

Squat down when speaking to child
Greet child and tell him about the activities you have prepared for him in the classroom.

Don't expect an answer – unless you know the child.

Settle parent and child in classroom.

Sometimes children will go straight to an activity – sandpit – water-play, etc.

Other children need to remain with parent and watch what is going on.

Most children under two will only be happy to play if they don't lose sight of their parent. Best way to interest child in an activity is to start doing it yourself.

If child or children start to do something you don't want them to, eg throwing sand, play it cool – don't laugh or draw attention to it – say no firmly and distract child with an alternative activity – it may work!

Most young children play on the floor – get down with them.

Talk to the child about what he is doing: it will extend his vocabulary, eg you are dribbling the sand through your fingers, the dough feels squashy, the water is trickling through the holes, etc.

Be aware: notice anything that needs doing – child who needs help on a climbing frame – help with mixing paint – parent who looks lonely, etc.

Tasks

You can do these in any order.

Involve yourself in an activity a child or children are doing

Talk to the parent about their child using prepared questionnaire

Record *ten-minute observation of one child* and add your comments on what you have observed.

Record your playgroup observation: note what you have learned from your observations.

Add any comments about your experience or intepretations of what you observed, eg 'I saw Jimmy snatch a spade that Mary was using – he is only 18 months and cannot be expected to have learned to share or take turns'.

Guide to Playgroups

Questions to ask parents – this should be a dialogue

Name of child

Age

Description
Mary has blue eyes, freckles on her nose and dimples when she smiles

Physical development
Weight, height, number of teeth, motor skills

Family
Mary lives with her mother and father and her two brothers who are 5 or 6 or 8

Home
Mary lives in a two-bedroomed flat – house – in a built-up area near a park
Safety considerations
Babysitting arrangements

Daily routine
Getting up, going to bed, mealtimes, what bed-time routine is followed

Play
What play activities does she like?
What toys does she have?
Which ones does she play with the most?
How does she use them?
Who does she play with?
Where does she play?
Does she have any opportunities for messy play?

Emotional development
Does she have a comforter?
Has she learned to share?
Take turns?
Say please and thank you?
Be happy playing out of sight of Mum?
Does she have temper tantrums?
What triggers them?
How is she dealt with?
Any naughty behaviour?
What fear does she have?
What makes her happy?

Television
Which programmes does she watch?
Which does she enjoy most?

Books
Which books does she have?
When does·she have stories read?

Health
Inoculations
Infectious illnesses:
    mumps; measles; German measles; chicken pox; tonsilitis, etc
What are the symptoms of any illnesses she has had?
What treatment did she have?
What *special* care is taken of her when she is unwell?
How does she behave when she is unwell?

Any other information

Record your findings.

Playgroup: focus on behaviour

Research data from adults:

1   Temper tantrums
Ask for an example of a temper tantrum.
How old was the child?
Where did it happen?
What triggered it?

Were there other contributing factors, eg child was
   Tired
   Hungry
   Bored
   Over excited
   Needed attention
   Couldn't make himself understood.
How did the child behave during the tantrum?
How did the adult feel?
What way did the adult react? (ask why they chose a course of action)
How was the situation resolved?

2   Mischief
What was the naughtiest thing a child had done?
How old was he?
Did he know he was being naughty?
How did the adult respond?
What effect did the response have on the child?

3   Naughty behaviour
Ask for examples of:
   Disobedient behaviour
   Destructive
   Aggressive.
How old was the child?
Place in the family, personality characteristics?
Ask adult to describe the incident?
What did he think motivated the child?
Ask adult how he felt?
Ask adult how the child felt?
What was the adult's reaction?
How was it resolved?
What do you think the child learned from the incident?
Add your comments

Observe *one* child.
Record in detail what he does during the time of observation.
Comment on how you think he is feeling.
What is he learning?
What contact does he make during the time with adults – mum or other adults
   in group, with children.

EXAMPLE
Playgroup
Here are some observations at a playgroup by a student focusing on play.

Laura and Jessica are just two years old and are twins. They have no brothers and sisters.

With what kind of things they play

Jessica and Laura both enjoy being read to and looking at books. They look at the pictures and love the colours. They look at the people in the stories and like to sit down and have their Mum read to them. Jessica took to a plastic doll in the nursery. You could see she liked to carry her doll around with her, just like her Mum carried her when she was a tiny baby.

Only just recently, Jessica's and Laura's Mum told us they had been getting very fond of water. They were fascinated by its movement and how it felt. They loved to watch it glisten and thought it was great fun to play in the wet. When they came into the playgroup the first thing they noticed was the water bath. Because they love water so much, their Mum told us that they adored having a bath. They loved to splash about and bang down on the water to watch it spray about them and up into their faces. But as they were still young, they couldn't quite understand the volume of water. If they took two bottle tops, one big one and one small and filled the large up with water, they couldn't quite understand why the smaller one overflowed when the big one's water was poured in it.

In the playground they liked the paints and the slide. They took some paints and sploshed them onto the paper. Although we couldn't really recognise what the picture was, they could. The slide really fascinated Jessica. She liked to try to climb up herself although she couldn't quite manage it and needed some help. Jessica had to take the doll she'd grown fond of with her, making sure that no one would take it when she wasn't looking. She knew it would be safe with her.

They also took a great liking to the sand. Their Mum told us that sand was too messy to have at home so when they saw it, it was like a special treat. They felt it with their hands and threw it. They watched it slither through their fingers when they hadn't let go. They poured it into their jugs and buckets, then tipped it out again, it was all a big adventure.

Both Jessica and Laura loved fitting things into things. They liked putting men in cars and pouring beans into cups. They loved to do things but found it quite difficult, especially with small objects.

For Christmas they got a 'Fisherman's Play Village' between them. They absolutely loved this as it had so much in it for them to do. It has shops and houses, fences and walls just like a real village does. They loved this and their Mum told us it was one of their best toys.

They love to jump in their cots, bouncing about. This is physical play. They move their whole bodies as they jump. They have discovery play, like playing in the sink and bath, throwing their toys and feeling water and sand. They have manipulative play, although they aren't yet very good. They did this when they fitted men in cars and played with lego and bricks. Jessica played imaginative play when she played with her doll, holding and dressing it like her Mum did to her when she was a tiny baby.

With whom they play

Jessica and Laura were only just starting to play with each other. They were not very friendly towards each other when they played and snatched and slapped each other when either Jessica or Laura had something the other wanted. Their Mum told me that her friend also had twins and she brought them to play with Laura and Jessica but they didn't yet all play together, or share their toys. They played with their Mum a lot and preferably those who were close to them, like uncles or aunties, all mostly adults.

How they felt when they played

When they played they felt different, depending when, where, what and with whom they played. Their Mum told us that they get frustrated if they try and do something and it does not work. But if they draw something nice, or build a tower in lego they feel happy. They feel pleased with themselves and glad they have succeeded. This is all very good as it teaches them to try hard and try again.

What they learn from play

Play teaches children everything. It teaches them to learn and pay attention, to share and to mix their feelings with others, it helps them to grow up and mature and it teaches them about the world around them. In a way it prepares them for when they are older.

They also learn a lot from each other, through play. They copy what each other does and also their Mum. Their vocabulary is the same as they learn their words by copying their Mum and each other. Their Mum tries to teach them to share but she knows they will both learn in time.

Here is a project undertaken by a student.

Why did playgroups start?

Playgroups started in the 1950s after the Second World War. Doctors said that the child learns more in his/her first five years, than in any time of his/her life. In the beginning of the playgroups mothers used to have them in their houses, as they couldn't afford the building and facilities.

The value of playgroups

The children themselves learn a great deal from the playgroups.
(a)   They get used to other people.
(b)   They learn to share.
(c)   They get confident to play with other children.
(d)   They adapt to other people's ways of life.

Benefits for mother

A mother can do a lot of things without the child pestering her and taking her time up. So a playgroup can:

(a) Give her a free morning.
(b) Get her involved with the playgroups.
(c) Give her fresh ideas to do at home
(d) Make new friends
(e) Talk with other people about their problems.

Also this benefits the child's day.

Playgroup activities
In some playgroups there is a noisy end and a quiet end.

Noisy end
A commando exercise course is put up which consists of tyres, ladders, chairs, etc. There are no serious injuries as a *child will know his/her limits*. You should never interfere with the child when he/she is playing or experimenting.

Quiet end
This is where painting and reading is mainly done. Children are allowed to do what they want, but there are exceptions. Teachers and parents must show interest in the children's work or they will lose their pride; also you must talk to the children and listen when required.

In a playschool they have certain facilities in parts of the room.

Home corner/Wendy House
Dressing-up corner. (This is where the imagination comes in, eg how to dress.)

Collage and models
They are using their imagination to make something become real. They use paper, material, and anything which can be used to make a collage, eg food, forestry stuff, flowers, necessities at home, and sea-shells.

Musical instruments
They learn basic rhythms. Learn from loud to soft and teacher must watch and listen. They learn actions to songs and also you must involve the restless children more.

The quality of parenting

Nothing is ever forgotten: the way a child is nursed, loved, spoken to, smiled at, establishes his feelings about himself and the people around him and can influence his whole future life. A child is not born with the ability to love, he has to learn it. Recent research indicates that this learning already begins in the womb. A baby whose parents are joyfully anticipating his arrival and are happy with each other are likely to transmit an awareness of love to the child in the womb. Sadly, if the mother is unhappy about having the baby, feelings of rejection will also be transmitted.

The best recipe for a happy, balanced and secure child is:
Two parents who care about each other, and understand each other
Accept the child as an individual
Enjoy the mutual responsibility of taking care of the child
Are willing to be flexible and adaptable to the changing needs of the child
Think ahead about practical considerations eg safety, balanced diet, routine, regular bedtimes, etc.

All these are essential parts of the quality of parenting. Without them the adult and child will be adrift, steering erratically for the dark shore of self-doubt and insecurity.

Children who are well cared for physically but are deprived of love do not thrive; they do not grow as tall or develop as well mentally and emotionally as children who are frequently touched, smiled at and whose presence and activities give visible joy to the people about them.

The following sections of the book provide a guide to the child's growth, the changing pattern of influence, learning and stimulation that is required to foster a rich texture of life. But none of this can happen without the quality of parenting I have described. All children need – personal loving, tender care; without it serious damage may be done to the development of their personality and they will not reach their potential.

Quality of parenting – thinking and learning about it
1 The author says that a child needs the following to become happy, balanced and secure:

Parents who accept the child as an individual, are willing to be flexible and adaptable to the needs of the child.

In small groups discuss what this means in practice – that is what parents have to do to show they are accepting the child as an individual or are being flexible. Try to think of parents who are like this.

PART II

The First Year of Life

DANA'S BEDTIME RITUALS

When Dana goes to bed my dad or
who puts her to bed has to say:

Mummy loves you
Daddy loves you
Dawny loves you
Dean loves you
   and Darren loves you.

My dad has to stroke her face at
the same time. Then she gives him
her right hand, stroking the back
of it she says:

Night, night
God bless
Love you
Then she changes hands and says, see you in the morning.

The birth experience

Nature, in her wisdom, makes the baby's journey and arrival into the world contrast dramatically with the previously tranquil existence. The walls of the womb suddenly close in, exerting a downward pressure and there is no respite from this. The baby makes his first contact with texture other than liquid, when the fluid drains. The head is used as a battering ram to penetrate the barrier and the skull is squeezed downwards through the birth canal, the pressure causing the head to become elongated in the process. That is why in the skull there are spaces – the **fontanelles** – which allow the bones of the skull to shift a little during its tight journey, where there is enough space, but only just enough.

The emerging baby has to breathe for the life support system is peeling off and the task is finished. The baby's lungs have never expanded before, the skin is new, used only to the feel of water on it. The baby has been propelled from the warm, dark and rhythmic capsule into a world of light and harsh sounds and multiple sensations. If the child is to breathe easily the nose and mouth must be cleared of amniotic fluid and mucous. It is routine for new babies to have this fluid sucked from them by tubes – but this can't feel good to the baby. To give birth, to use the words of Judy, one of the mothers I spoke to 'is sensational'. For the baby too it must be just that – sensationally disturbing. What the baby most needs after the traumatic journey and the first independent breath is to rest and to find comfort. The baby has been inside the mother and forced out from her and now she must take the child to her. Indeed, she is programmed to do so, for what she wants most of all is to lift the baby and place the child against her. Those first moments of life, the very first experience of independent life can never be forgotten. They must stay as part of us for always. To put the baby to the breast, to suck and find a new form of contact and security, is to establish for the new human being an awareness of love and care. To deprive the child of this is to emphasise the desolation felt and offer no comfort.

For a couple the birth of their child is the most momentous and important event of their lives. They have become parents and as parents they are now in charge of a unique human individual whose needs are complex. In order to begin to understand their baby they must first recognise their own reactions to this change in their lives. Neither of them will ever again function as a separate individual – for from now on they will begin to experience pain and pleasure that is not their own. If their child is unhappy they cannot be joyful; if their child is hungry they must do something to satisfy that hunger. I was once asked by a young woman when talking about these very developed feelings of concern that parents feel for their children – 'when do you stop feeling this way towards your children?' Obviously when they are helpless and totally dependent on us for their well being, these emotions are at their most powerful, but they never altogether cease. Women cannot come to terms with this colossal change without the need for some adjustment to be made. After the elation has passed, when the sense of achievement has had time to abate, the mother's bodily chemistry is changing and she experiences what most people refer to as 'the fourth-day blues'. Suddenly everything is grey, she feels trapped, inadequate, different and fears arrive. Asked why she is crying she can rarely give a specific reason but normally sympathy from the father and a caring attitude from those around her will be sufficient to dispel the depression.

In the labour ward women come together from all different places in society and for a short time they are bonded together by their common experience of childbirth.

Although a stay in any institution is made irritating by rules and routines which are not of one's choosing, these should not be allowed to over-shadow the more positive aspects of the situation. The togetherness that newly delivered mothers can become part of in a maternity ward has many benefits. At this time all the barriers are down and women can open up and talk to each other about everything, each adding to the other's pool of knowledge. Not only can they learn from each other and the nursing staff how to handle their baby, but they can discuss what they experienced at birth. This also becomes a time when women will talk about the most intimate aspects of their lives, frank discussion about sex or their most hidden fears and wishes are openly confided. Each learns from the other, just like the past, when giving birth was an altogether female experience involving all those close to the mother. Now this can be recaptured in a different setting, for, after giving birth, women once again find themselves together and can, as before, give mutual support.

Check your learning   The birth experience

1   The author says the mother is 'programmed' to lift the new-born baby and place the child against her. Can you work out, by going over the text if necessary, why this should be so important in nature?

2   Explain fully what the author means when she writes of parents: 'Neither of them will ever again function as a separate individual . . .' (page 59).

3   What causes 'fourth-day blues' and what can be done to help by members of the family?

4   Explain what is the advantage of a labour ward mentioned above.

The new baby

After birth the first urgent question is: 'How's the baby?' and in most cases the answer is an unqualified 'fine', but inevitably the parents always seek reassurance, asking: 'Does the baby have the correct number of limbs, fingers and toes? Are the lungs working and his heart beating?' When a baby sounds a first cry there is relief and joy for everyone in the delivery room. What the mother most wants to do is to hold her baby. She needs to be able to touch and explore the baby's body, to see for herself that her child is perfect. She has carried the baby inside, but has seen nothing; she has felt the baby move, but has not touched anything. When the child is at last born, her need to handle the baby is all-impelling.

The first minutes that the parents share with their new baby are very important. The baby at birth is immediately given to the mother and often the mother is encouraged to put the baby straight to her breast. After the turmoil of the birth the baby suckling at the breast makes for a calming atmosphere in which the mother and child can establish their relationship. Research has now proved that a mother who cuddles her baby after the birth is more likely to have a close loving relationship with the child later on.

Once the first contacts between the new baby and his parents has been successfully made, the next step is that the mother can be washed and made comfortable and the parents enjoy a cup of tea while the baby is examined more fully. There will be checks on limbs and on the face. The spine will be looked at to make sure that there is no swelling which might indicate that the child has been born with spina bifida. The doctor or midwife will also look for any signs of Down's Syndrome – a condition which used to be called mongolism – and the mouth will be examined to check for cleft pallet.

A special test has been devised called the **Alogar score**, named after the American doctor who created it. Each baby is assessed on the Alogar score: which is a special rating that gives an overall measure of the baby's well being. Points are given for factors like breathing and heart rate, the way the baby responds to stimulations, the state of the muscles and the colour of his skin. This test usually shows at once whether there is any need for concern. The paediatrician, a doctor who is an expert in infant and child health, will also see the baby and at a later stage do more detailed checks.

The mother may need to have stitches if an episiotomy (a cut made in the vagina) has been done. When these are completed she will be taken to the maternity ward and usually has a good sleep. The father is left with the task of informing all the relatives and friends that their child has been born.

The baby is placed in a cot next to the mother's bed. It is best for mother and her baby not to be separated, for the period after birth is an especially sensitive one for helping mother and baby to get to know each other and make their relationship easier to establish. Not all mothers feel a surge of love for their babies. For some mothers this only happens after a period of time during which, by handling and feeding their babies, they grow to love them. Unfortunately, sometimes it is unavoidable to separate the mother and baby at birth because the baby will only thrive if expert care in a special care unit is given. Babies that need this extra care are ones who are born too soon or have low birth weight. A baby weighing less than 2kg at birth falls into this category.

Babies needing special care

Some babies have trouble in breathing or because they have been born too early, their lungs are not mature enough to breathe normally. Other babies need the controlled warmth and humidity provided by the incubator to keep their body temperature steady. Babies who have had some problems during delivery, such as foetal distress, are also taken into the special care unit for observation. Babies delivered by Caesarian section are also kept under special care for a short time. The unfortunate babies who have been born with some malformation are taken care of in the special unit. Jaundice is a common problem with pre-term babies and can be easily cured. The yellow colouring of the skin is caused by an excess of a chemical called *bili rabin* but by putting the baby under ultra violet light the chemical can be broken down and the jaundice cleared. Generally this condition means that the liver is a little slower than average in developing.

A baby arriving for observation needs to be nursed naked in an incubator. Premature babies, (babies who are born before 37 completed weeks), may not have learned how to suck so they cannot feed from breast or bottle and need to be tube-fed. In these cases, a tube is passed down their nostril and into the stomach and milk is poured down it. These babies are given a dummy to suck when they are being fed so that they come to associate being fed with sucking. Very sick babies receive food through a drip into a vein.

Mothers take part in caring for their babies as soon as they are able. Nurses explain what the various pieces of machinery are used for and the doctors inform the mother and father about any treatments they prescribe and about the progress the baby is making. It is all important for the parents to be fully informed about the condition of their child and to feel that they are involved in any decisions taken by the doctor. If there is something wrong with the baby, mothers and fathers cope much better with having the facts about the baby's condition explained to them, rather than having to grapple alone with their unspoken fears.

The new baby – what have we learned?

1   In your own words write all you know about the Alogar test.
2   What is a paediatrician?
3   What job is suggested the father can do when the new mother goes back to the ward for a good sleep?
4   Below what weight are babies looked after in the special care unit?
5   List the things mentioned which mean that a baby needs special care.
6   What is foetal distress?
7   What causes jaundice? How can it be cleared? What effect may it have on the development of the liver?
8   Define a premature baby.
9   The author says parents should be told about anything wrong with the baby. Why is this?

Breast feeding

The reason women have breasts is so they can feed their babies. During pregnancy the breasts undergo changes which prepare them for their task of milk production. In the ante-natal clinic the midwives will teach mothers how to keep their nipples supple and, after the birth, mothers will be given advice and encouragement in how to establish successful breast feeding.

There is no doubt that breast milk is the best food for the human baby; it is made by the mother's body specifically for the baby so it suits the child's needs exactly. The baby can be put to the breast right from birth. For the first three days the breasts produce the same substance that has been made during pregnancy – a thick yellowish liquid called colostrum. This is very good for the baby because it contains the vital nourishment it needs as well as antibodies which help to protect the child against illness. When, on the third day, the milk arrives, it looks thinner than cows' milk and has a bluish tinge. But as well as providing a convenient and perfectly balanced diet, it also protects the baby from infection and disease. If a woman breast feeds she does it for free; it is always available in the right amount and at the correct temperature. Breast feeding can be one of the most rewarding aspects of motherhood as with breast feeding there is a warm, physical contact between mother and child. *Feeding from the baby's point of view is the most important event of his day* and the child receives a great deal of pleasure from feeding. Babies enjoy the act of sucking, especially combined with the warmth and security given by close contact to their mothers. Within a few days the baby may start to stare fixedly at his mother whilst feeding, focusing his eyes for the first time on her face and will be content. For the mother this can be a wonderful emotional and physical experience and it helps her to get her figure back more quickly.

Very occasionally babies die during the first year of life. Many of these deaths occur quite suddenly and for no apparent reason. Often they are referred to as cot deaths. These deaths are less frequent in breast-fed babies than those who have been bottle-fed. The cause of these tragedies is not known yet, but it is likely that many of them are due to sudden infections.

Not all women are able to breast feed and certainly many do not choose to do so. Some women find breast feeding embarrassing, particularly if their husband's attitude is unsure. Many feel that by chooseing to breast feed they tie themselves to the baby, while if they are bottle-fed someone else can always do it for them. Occasionally they are discouraged by over-keen grannies who would rather the mother bottle-fed so that they can also have a hand in it. Certainly, as a society we don't provide enough private arrangements for breast feeding in public places, so travelling on a train or shopping for a breast feeding mum can have problems. If a mother resumes work soon after the baby is born, she may find it difficult to continue breast feeding and may only be able to do it twice a day, morning and evening.

All milk that is not breast milk starts out as cows' milk and has to be chemically processed to be suitable for human babies. Because calves grow to maturity in eighteen months the protein content of cows' milk is much higher than human milk so is more difficult for the baby to digest. It also contains too much salt and the mother who bottle feeds should remember to give her baby drinks of boiled water as he will be more thirsty. Babies who are bottle-fed have hard stools and are more prone to constipation. Artificial milk can encourage the growth of harmful bacteria in the gut because it has less acid and doesn't contain any of the protective organisms found in breast milk. That is why a bottle-fed baby is more prone to gastro-enteritis.

Mothers bottle feeding their babies have to be very careful not to add 'one for the pot' when they are making up the feed, but should make up the exact amount, because if the feed is too concentrated it will disagree with the baby and there is also a danger of over-feeding. It usually happens when the feed is made up too concentrated. The concentrated feed makes the baby more thirsty and so the baby cries, the mother interprets this cry as hunger and gives him more milk. Fat babies may look cuddly, but they develop more slowly and are more prone to get ill or grow up into fat adults.

When bottle feeding the feeds have to be made up, bottles warmed and bottles, teats, jugs and anything else that is used have to be washed very carefully and sterilised. 'It is such a comfort to me to feed my son,' said one mother. She was holding her eleven month son in her arms, his face beaming, all smiles. 'I know it was very good for him and necessary as a food till he was six months, but after that it is more the emotional comfort you can provide on demand that is so rewarding. When he becomes really distressed I can make him content again and this gives me such a sense of relief and comfort to know I have been able to do that for him.'

If a mother is totally unable to breast feed then she should not despair or feel guilty and inadequate. Instead, she should give her child as much physical contact as a breast-feeding mother, ie spend as much time holding her baby. Then the child will feel close and secure.

What have I learned?   Breast feeding
1   Why is colostrum good for the new baby?
2   What are the advantages of human milk for the baby?
3   What is thought to be cause of cot deaths? Why are cot deaths mentioned in a section on breast feeding?
4   Why do some mothers prefer to use bottle feeding?
5   What are the disadvantages of using cows' milk for feeding a baby?
6   Why is it important to put in exactly the right amount of milk powder when making up a feed?
7   Apart from nutrition what does the mother give the baby when feeding? (Bottle or breast)

Birth to six weeks: development guide

Here is a progress check on what should occur during this period

A new-born baby sleeps most of the day and wakes only for feeds. He lies curled up and the head is very wobbly. The baby will turn towards bright lights and will become startled by loud noises. The baby will hold onto his mother's hair, fingers, etc, with a strong grasp.

Reflex actions
Rooting reflex
Walking reflex
The baby makes grunting noises. Week by week the baby will become more wakeful and when awake the baby must be played with. From three weeks onward the baby begins to focus and will recognise his mother's and father's face.

Four to eight weeks
The baby will give a first social smile.

Six weeks
At about six weeks the baby will 'coo' at friendly noises and attention, will sleep most of the time unless being fed or handled. By now the baby can focus clearly and will follow moving objects. If the cheek is touched, the baby will turn round to suck. The head is still wobbly but the baby can lift shoulders and head when lying on the stomach.

What the baby can feel
Hunger
Heat
Discomfort (the only way discomfort can be expressed is by crying)
Loneliness

Answer the baby's needs
You must always answer the baby's needs – you cannot spoil a new-born baby.

Things they don't like
Babies do not like loud irritating noises, and being handled by nervous people.

Help for the mother

When the baby is brought home, the mother must have somebody there to help her with the housework and shopping. She should be given all the time in the world to be with her baby. It is quite wrong to get someone to look after the baby so the mother can do the shopping and housework!

A routine

A mother must adopt some kind of routine for:
  Feeding times
  Bathing times
  Sleeping times
  and also she must allow herself time for:
    getting her own breakfast
    doing her household chores
    and just general time for herself and her relaxation.

Problems

A woman may feel very tired, she may wonder if she's doing the right thing, she will also feel depressed, tied down and restricted. If she feels inadequate she should go out or invite other mothers in to talk. But she must never let herself go, she needs to look good, so as to give herself confidence.

EXAMPLE

A student's recorded observation of a baby at six weeks

DEAN six weeks old
Birth weight: 3.5kg

Movement

Dean has an unco-ordinated movement. His reflex actions are: he has a very tight grip with his fingers. If you hold him by his hands he will do walking movements with his feet. He cannot hold his head up. Noise does not disturb him. He is quite content. He will do eye-to-eye contact with his mother.

Discomfort

At 5 weeks old Dean started to feel cold and discomfort – at that age he loses body heat quickly. He will get bored and lonely and needs physical attention and emotional needing attention. He will need clothing. Also he will want somebody to talk to him and love him.

Stimulation

If we put him on his belly, he will start to lift his head up and try to crawl.

Problems

Two problems that Dean's mother had was: waking up at night and getting wind up.

Change for mother

The mother is tied down and can't do so much planning. His father loves holding him and playing with him.

Making up bottles

Dean's mother uses a sterilising unit – it gets rid of all germs and it works in 30 minutes. Boil up water, measure 175g of Cow & Gate or your own choice of brand. That will be enough for five feeds a day. It takes about one hour to feed him.

Washing nappies

Dean's mother soaked his nappies in Nappisan – it gets rid of all germs.

Bath

He loves a bath and has one every night in a plastic bath for babies.

What have I learned?   Birth to six weeks

1   What is a reflex action?

2   Can you spoil a new-born baby?

3   Go through the description of Dean with someone else in the class and find all the things which are characteristic of a six-week-old baby.

4   Learn the facts given about a baby from birth to six weeks and with another member of the class test each other.

5   Why is it wrong for mother to get someone to look after the baby so she can do shopping and housework?

6   What does 'routine' mean and why are the routines mentioned so important?

Six months: development guide

Motor development
Lying on back, raises head to look at feet.
Sits with support in baby chair or pram.
Holds arms up to be lifted.
Hands held – pulls up to sit.
Kicks strongly.
Rolls over from front to back and perhaps also from back to front.
May sit unsupported for about 30 seconds before overbalancing.
Held standing – bears weight and bounces up and down.
Holds with whole hand and passes small objects from one hand to another.

Visual development
Very alert and interested. Moves head and eyes eagerly in every direction, when attention is attracted.
Eyes move together. Any sign of a squint should now be investigated.
Attention fixes on a face or object ahead and the baby reaches out to grasp it.
When a toy falls and remains within sight, the baby will watch it fall and come to rest.
If the toy falls out of sight, the baby will forget about it.

Hearing and speech
Responds immediately to mother's voice in room – turning towards her.
Babbles to self – sing song vowel sounds, and repetitive sounds, eg dddd or bbbb.
Laughs, chuckles, squeaks in play.
Responds to different tone of mother's voice – pleased, annoyed, unhappy.

Play
Reaches out and grasps toy/small object. Usually with both hands.
Takes everything to mouth.
Plays with feet and hands, finds them very interesting.
Puts hands to bottle/cup and pats it while feeding.
Will shake a rattle deliberately to make a sound – watching it closely at the same time.
Still friendly with strangers, but may show some shyness or even anxiety, especially if mother is out of sight.

Interested in cause and effect, eg bangs on table with wooden block; squeezes
  rubber toy for the squeak; scratches carpet or chair cover and listens to the
  noise made. Repeats action again and again.
Six months is the usual time for cutting tooth (lower incisor). Important to have
  good food at this stage.

Feeding
Can have cows' milk and vitamin drops.
Begins to use cup.
Breast-fed babies can be weaned straight on to cows' milk from cup without
  ever having bottle.
Sieved or puréed foods from spoon – tins, jars or home cooking – easily
  digested, nourishing savoury foods are best.
Sweet foods and cereals should be avoided – fattening, decay teeth and provide
  little or no nourishment.
Three meals per day.
Routine and pattern for day to fit in with family routine.
At six months the baby should have doubled his birth weight.

EXAMPLE

A student's recorded observation of a baby at six months
On Friday Mrs Jones came in to see us with the Health Visitor and her six-
month-old baby boy, LEE.

Physical development
Lee is a very happy baby and does not cry much. This is because his needs
are satisfied. It is very important to respond to everything the baby needs
in his first year. If he is hungry then feed him, if he cries – pick him up. If
you respond to him then the child feels secure in the knowledge that he is
loved and wanted. If baby's needs are not responded to the baby will
become unhappy and nervous.

Lee can now sit alone momentarily, although he does not have firm
control he has a steady head. When he lies on his tummy he can lift his
chest off the floor and turn from one side to the other. Babies learn to
move backwards and sidewards before they crawl.

Lee has clear skin and eyes and he is bright and alert. He can move his
eyes to follow an object. He can follow sound and can grasp things with
the palm of his hand. He can transfer things from one hand to the other
and can reach out, he now has more *co-ordination*. At this age he is
beginning to examine things in a more mature way. He responds to
speech by coo-ing and bubbling noises. By six months babies should
have doubled their birthweight, but although Lee has gone more than that

he is not overweight. It is bad for babies to be overweight because they have breathing problems and are too heavy for their legs. Babies shouldn't squint anymore, they should look clearly at things. Their hands are now mostly open.

Skills and social responses
Lee can now smile and laugh and enjoy being held, looked at and talked to. He is now beginning to copy.

Information given by the Health Visitor

Food
At four months the baby can be started on solid foods. They can be fed on liquidised or puréed foods with no lumps. Mothers are encouraged to give savoury foods not sweet ones as the way you are fed when you are a baby will influence whether or not you are healthy and have good strong teeth. If the baby does not get to expect sweet foods he will not need them.

Introduce solid foods gradually with a variety of tastes, eg puréed vegetables and potatoes, small quantities of meat and fruit. No sugar. Rice-based cereals. At six months the baby can chew, although he has no teeth his gums are hard. He can now begin to take things finely chopped and cows' milk. When starting a baby on cows' milk you should add one-third water in case of allergies. One pint of milk a day is enough.

Safety in the home
Baby is now beginning to move very quickly. It is important to take the following precautions:
Fire guard
Plug guards
Gate for stairs
Cooker guard

In the kitchen:
Bleaches etc should be moved out of the way to high cupboards along with glassware, pills, medicine and tablets.
Electric kettle leads should be kept well out of the way or a nasty accident could occur involving the baby getting scalded.

Inoculations
Nearly all babies between the age of three and eleven months need to be immunised against:
Diphtieria
Whooping cough
Tetanus
Polio

What have I learned?   The six months old and one year old child

1   When you have carefully studied the six-month-old baby and read the student's description of Lee, plan and write your own description of a six-month-old child – in your own words – which includes as much of the information given as possible. The teacher will tell you whether it can be a real child or a made-up one or either.

2   When you have read the one-year-old child section and the description of Mark Platt, do the same as you did in question 1. This time there will be more about the home and toys.

The one year old: development guide

In the months between six and twelve the baby will have learned new skills:
Sits alone – average age of seven months.
Crawls – average age of eight/nine months.
Picks up with finger and thumb – much finer movement for smaller objects.
Deliberately drops or throws things at eight/nine months.
Babbles in 'conversation', often very earnestly.
Shouts to attract attention, rather than crying.
Should have had hearing tested and have started immunisations.

One year
By this time, sits alone easily.
Crawls.
Pulls up to stand, and walks around furniture.
May walk – normal range for first steps – 9/18 months. Average 13 months.
May crawl upstairs – needs safety stair gate.

Understanding
Knows own name.
Understands simple questions or commands, eg 'No' 'Where's daddy?' 'Give it
to me.'
Says a handful of words – usually 'Mum' 'Dad' 'Bye, bye' etc.

Development of understanding through play
Loves toys that make a noise.
Plays with simple toys, eg bricks, graded beakers, learning about size, shape
and interrelationships.
Loves to put things into containers and take them out again. Finds a toy hidden
before his eyes.
Begins to show an interest in pictures. Will enjoy a simple picture book if shared
with mother.
Always exploring and experimenting.
Throws, rolls, pushes, bangs and bounces.
Watches where and how things fall.
Plays with water at bathtime, tries to pick it up and hold it, or to push sponge
under the water and watch it bob up.

Enjoys repetition – discovering and confirming the cause and effect.

Loves little simple songs or nursery rhymes.

Loves clapping hands and playing pat-a-cake or peek-a-boo.

Generous – will offer playthings but may, at the last minute, be unable to part with it.

Especially loves real objects – boxes of all shapes and sizes, saucepans, plastic containers, etc. Can open boxes and undo screw-tops. Dangerous substances, eg medicines, tablets and household cleaners should be put out of reach and locked away.

Affectionate to those known
Usually wary of strangers.

Knows people exist even when they cannot be seen.

Loves to play with a loved adult or older child – playing together, eg on carpet – rolling, crawling together and 'rough and tumble'.

Needs lots of play and cuddles
Bathtime can be fun – splashing about and a good time for a sing song.

Attachment to mother
As it is usually mother who is there all day, the baby is most dependent on her. Some babies are by nature more dependent than others but past experience plays a large part. If the baby feels insecure, perhaps because of past separations, the child is likely to be more dependent, through fear of losing the mother.

Management of one year old
Can get about at will.

Does not know which things are toys and which are forbidden.

Move things which are breakable and dangerous.

Try to avoid inconsistency, eg not allowing baby to touch TV buttons, but another time letting him play with them to keep the peace. This confuses. A baby will return to forbidden objects. Always say 'No' firmly and give some simple explanation.

A one year old is very mobile, interested and inquisitive – frustration leads to angry outbursts. May have restrictions eg being strapped into pushchair. Try to divert attention.

Needs lots of patience and humour
If sleeping problems develop – tire out during the day, mentally and physically.

Feeding – family food, pint of milk daily. Vitamins.

Drinks unaided from a cup. Chews. Feeds with fingers. Holds spoon and bangs.

	MARCH LTRS	APRIL LTRS	MAY LTRS
25			
42	33	3	17
30	70	30	25
25			
72	103	33	42
			3924
939			1660
			3924
939			1660
4192	2840	3443	9950
4042	6215	7984	18469

EXAMPLE

A student's recorded observation of Mark at one year

Mrs Platt and her son, Mark, ten months

Description
Mark is one year old and is very chubby in appearance. He very much enjoyed feeling the sand, and picking it up and putting it on the floor. He then swept the sand over the floor and gave a little grin as if to say 'look what I've done, aren't I clever?'

Toys
Now that Mark is crawling he very much likes to play with moving toys such as tricycles and push-along animals, etc. He also likes noisy toys and Mrs Platt is considering buying him a Xylophone for Christmas, so that he can bang at it. Mark has a small play area in the corner of the living room, he usually plays in here for twenty minutes at a time. This gives Mrs Platt a little time to put her feet up – but her eyes of course have to be on Mark. When Mark was born he was given a big Teddy Bear which he has only just noticed. He now cuddles it and hits it when 'it is naughty'. Bruno the bear has become very special to him. He finds books very interesting and gets terribly excited when he is shown one.

Communicating
As Mark can't talk yet he has to find another way of communicating. He can't point so he has to use his whole body to express what he wants. If he wants to get down from his mum's lap he has to wriggle down because he can't say what he wants or even point to it.

Safety
You always have to be one step in front of a child because every day he masters new skills such as opening cupboards and doors, climbing off chairs and being able to screw lids off containers. These things you never know he can do until you see him doing them – he doesn't tell you. You need to be on your guard all the time, you never know what he's going to do next.

Mrs Platt has made many alterations to her home since having Mark. She has moved all of her ornaments and anything of value. She has special plastic plugs which fit into the electric sockets so that Mark can't electrocute himself. There used to be a pan rack in the kitchen but now that has been moved because Mark pulls it over. The kettle is on its own special shelf but Mrs Platt does admit that the lead does hang down sometimes which could be fatal if Mark managed to pull at it. Mrs Platt never lets Mark out of her sight – she even takes him to the toilet with her. He plays in the bath with his toys. Mrs Platt never does ironing when Mark is around because it is far too dangerous. Mrs Platt has had to clear both bedside tables in her bedroom because Mark comes into bed with her and her husband and he has a tendancy to pick up things and bite them. This causes another problem as Mr Platt likes to have a drink of water with him during the night – in the morning Mark tries to bite the glass. This could also not only be very dangerous but fatal.

There is a safety gate at the top of the stairs but not at the bottom because he can't get to them.

Every day Mark masters some new skill – the most recent one was being able to open cupboards – now Mrs Platt will have to fix locks onto all her cupboards.

Mrs Platt used to keep all of her cleaning equipment in a cupboard in the bathroom, but when Mark begun to undo cupboards she moved them to a cupboard in the kitchen – then she realised that this was just as silly.

They have central heating so they don't have a fire guard. The fire is only ever on when Mark is in bed. The problem is that a babysitter wouldn't know this and may have the fire on whilst Mark is around.

Mrs Platt has to be very careful when she takes Mark to his grandparents' house – because they have no safety equipment at all. This must be very frustrating for Mark as he is not allowed away from his Mum.

One day not very long ago Mark gave a very loud scream, so Mrs Platt realised that he must have been in pain. Later when changing Mark she found a peanut in Mark's nappy. This had caused the scream. He must have picked it up from the floor – Mrs Platt had had guests round the night before, so it must have been dropped then.

Personal points

I noticed that during the lesson Mrs Platt gave Mark a plastic protective electric point cover to play with. I thought this was very stupid because if one day Mrs Platt was in a hurry she might not push the cover right in. Mark could see this and thinking that Mummy gave it to him to play with, may pull or try to pull it out. Chances are he may electrocute himself.

Guide to toilet training

When the child has reached 18 months toilet training can begin.
Take nappies off and put in trainer pants, gentle reminders.

How children learn to talk

The child's first exposure to sound and language is in the womb. From there can be heard the beating of the mother's heart, the gurgling of her stomach and the sound of her voice – which is a familiar and comforting sound. Children bring a sense of rhythm from the womb, where, for nine months the most dominant sound in their lives was the mother's heartbeat.

When the baby is born, the tone of voice used by the mother tells the child what to expect, even though the words cannot be understood. Babies can listen to and understand 'cross' sounds, 'food' sounds and 'happy' sounds. The baby uses sight, touch, and hearing to obtain meaning from sound.

Talking is a difficult feat, which needs special mouth movements. These *mechanics* must be practised in order for a child to learn to talk. Sucking, chewing and licking all helps to develop these vital mouth movements.

If a child uses a dummy or sucks a thumb, then ensure this does not become excessive or there is a danger of not exploring the rest of the mouth which could later produce speech problems.

Baby play is also an important part of developing children's speech. Babies like being tickled and bounced and this encourages them to laugh which in turn encourages them to express happiness. Baby play is also valuable because as the adults play they also talk which exposes the child to language.

Development of speech
At *six weeks* a baby should be making throaty, chewing noises made up of a mixture of different sounds. The child should also be responding to voices of every day noises.

At *seven to eight months* the baby should be gurgling. This is called pre-lingual speech and is a fore-runner of the true use of words.

If by *ten months* the child is not 'babbling' repetitively the doctor should be consulted.

First words and sentences
At *nine to ten months* a child should make the first meaningful sounds such as 'Da-Da' or 'Ma-Ma'. If grown-ups continually repeat these sounds then it gives the child the incentive to repeat them. By parents reacting and repeating these words a child is taught the meaning to these naturally produced words. This principle also applies to animal sounds. Sounds such as 'meow', and 'quack-quack' help the child to identify them with the animals to which the sounds correspond.

At the *end of the first year* the child should be using single words for communication. The child will put names to things and repeat sounds and words. Soon two or more words will be fused together, eg goodboy, allgone.

The baby will use single words as complete sentences, eg 'I want to go out'.

Once the child has a basic stock of words, two or three word sentences are used with only the important words, eg 'Throw ball' or 'Baby crying'.

By the age of two and a half or three the foundations of language are usually firmly established. Typical first words from some of the children studied were:

Ball	Ta	Biscuit
Sea	What?	Duck
Baby	Nan	Shoe
Drink	Pus-pussy?	Car
Down	Bird	Whatsdat
Book	Dad	Mum
		No

Children usually make few *grammatical mistakes* but sometimes they will learn, for example, a proper past tense such as 'brought' and then later change it to an improper past tense such as 'bringed' or 'brang'.

Talking is a big step forward in every child's life; it changes the way they see, feel and think. As the child learns more words the concepts of shapes and space become clarified. *Concept words* should be used, eg: colour, long, heavy, etc, when talking to a child to help explain these words and ideas.

Toddlers know time-related words, eg night, day, now, first, but may mix up yesterday, today and tomorrow. They may also choose one word to mean any point in the past or future time, such as tonight.

Children may use words in the wrong context, eg 'a heavy slope' when they mean a slope which is hard to walk up.

When having a conversation with children of this age adults should strive to repeat words, expand their meanings, make their sentences more accurate and use action words, eg ran, jumped, yelled.

Promoting speech

Talking sheds light on everyday ideas. It also helps strengthen the bond between mother and child as they discuss their feelings and thoughts.

In the last section I discussed the different stages of development in speech. In order to develop a child's speech in the best way, action should be taken from birth:

One of the most important activities is **reading**. Books help children associate actions with words and make them understand that symbols on a page have a meaning and that meaning is associated with spoken sounds. Books will also provide a wider vocabulary and an opportunity to memorise and repeat words and phrases.

By teaching the child **nursery rhymes and songs** the adult is helping them to understand words. Because they like the rhythm and rhymes they will memorise them and try to repeat them.

All parents take their children on **outings** and this is the perfect time for learning. It gives the child an opportunity to ask questions and the adult can get feed-back from children about experiences. For example, going to the zoo the child can learn about animals, other people, transportation (going to and from the zoo), etc . . .

Creative play such as drawing, painting, using sticky paper, as well as clay and dough is another important activity to develop speech. It encourages children to use words and sentences to explain and discuss their artisitic creations. Parents can also use their child's endeavours to discuss selected subjects, eg picture of a cat – discuss related subjects like the family cat or a neighbour's, or kittens, or tigers and lions, dogs, mice, softness, colour, etc.

Starting at about the age of three a child will begin playing with *other children*. Other children provide stimulus for communicating and conversation. If the child does not play with other children he may begin to talk at a later stage because parents tend to anticipate their child's needs while other children do not.

Direct speech is one of the more obvious means of promoting the child's speech development but that does not make it any the less important. The repeated rhythmic talk becomes familiar to a baby and the child repeats this as the years pass. Direct speech also provides a time for the child to ask questions and talk to the parents.

Indirect speech teaches the child new words whilst listening to other people talking. The child is encouraged to talk by hearing other people communicating.

Encouragement is a very important part of learning to speak and without it the child will have much more difficulty in learning. If the child's parents have a good attitude towards language development then the child is more likely to put more effort into learning to speak earlier. Encouragement also plays a part in all the other language developing activities and without it a child would never be able to accomplish anything.

Retarded speech development

Sometimes children do not learn to talk at the average age and these are some of the warning signals to watch out for:

By 6–8 weeks	baby not responding to voices of everyday sounds.
3–4 months	baby not babbling repetitively to self and playthings.
10 months	baby not babbling repetitively to self and others (average is 7–8 months).
21 months	baby not speaking single words (average is 13–15 months).
27 months	baby not putting two or three words together in short sentences (average is 18–22 months).
4 years	child not using fully intelligent speech (average is 3–3½ years).

If any of these signals apply to a baby you should take him to a doctor or speech therapist who will decide what has retarded your child's speech development.

This triangle shows the four things which must be present in order for a child to learn to talk:

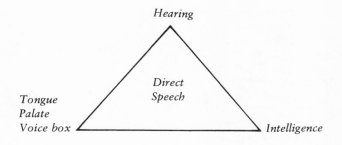

Hearing

*Direct
Speech*

*Tongue
Palate
Voice box*

Intelligence

Hearing should be tested at an early age and children *must* be talked to: children can be retarded for life if they do not hear enough speech in the first months of life. The greatest help in developing children's intellect is to let them hear abundant speech. Even if hearing, intelligence, and the tongue, palate, and voice box are all intact a child may still be prevented from talking because of a **trauma**. A trauma is an emotional scar which can cause a child to stop speaking, eg a two year old whose parents are both killed in a car crash might stop talking from shock. A child I know spent time in hospital in traction after an accident, she was very distressed by the experience and her language development was halted. Twins will almost always learn to talk later than average. This is because they spend more time together than with their parents – and they will use a private code of noises, movement and gesture.

If a child has to be taken to a speech therapist there are many paths the therapist can take in relation to the problem the child has. Here are two examples:

Rebecca is two but all she can say is 'mummy' and 'no'. Her hearing and understanding were both found to be good when tested but she had a lag between hearing and talking. She needs to understand words as a symbol and a code so the therapist has her playing with miniature toys (doll's furniture) which are a code for the real word. She is improving. Ben is about the same age but he cannot pronounce certain sounds. As a baby, Ben never learnt the correct mechanics so he is learning them now. One of the things the therapist did was to make Ben reach with his tongue a cherry placed on his upper lip. This made him enjoy the exercise that his tongue needed.

Speech is a very important part of life and without it the world can become a hostile and confusing place. In most cases it is in the hands of the parents to promote this very important side of life and they should do all they can to encourage and guide the child. Once the child can talk babyhood is over. The child can ask questions, talk, sing, and make known what is wanted – rather than crying for it. This new world for the child must be opened up by the parent.

Reading to children is a very important part of their experience and it should start as early as possible.

What have I learned?   How children learn to talk

1   What does the child learn from the *tone* of a mother's voice?

2   Why are sucking and chewing important in learning to talk and why is too much dummy- or thumb-sucking a bad thing?

3   What is the importance of play, especially tickling, in learning to talk?

4   With another member of the class test yourself on the development of speech from 6 weeks to 10 months.

5   Explain the meaning of 'concept word'.

6   How will the toddler talk about time?

7   How can adults best encourage the development of talk when themselves speaking to children?

8   The author writes about eight ways action can be taken to help develop a child's speech from birth. Using notes you made up after studying the text, give a short talk to a classmate telling him about these eight activities.

9   The best way to learn the signs of retarded speech development is doing your study of actual children.

10   Explain what a trauma is. How does it affect speech?

11   Why do twins often learn to talk late?

Work on children's books

The study of children's books moves the area of work from concentrating on the baby and takes the student into the world of children. Authors of children's books give valuable *insight* into what interests children – how they behave, what they are afraid of and how to prepare them for new experiences, etc.

Books for children provide a fascinating source of information *about* children, eg they show how children under the age of three enjoy books about everyday things because that is what they are gaining knowledge about, while the child from three onwards begins to have more diverse interests and experiences more complex emotions and the subject and content of children's books reflect this.

Children's stories help to illuminate the child for the student. At the same time students re-discover the pleasure of books enjoyed in their own childhood or find themselves discovering for the first time the fun and joy you can get from reading children's books. Hopefully they will pass on this discovery to their own children.

Why read to children?

Through stories children learn to identify, ie put themselves in the place of fictional characters and so understand themselves and others better. *My Naughty Little Sister* is a good example of such a book.

Reading books to children, singing nursery rhymes to them and telling them stories *undoubtedly enlarges the child's vocabulary*. It increases his 'power of speech'. This helps him to communicate his needs and feelings and express his growing awareness of the world firstly to his family and later to his friends, playgroup leaders, teachers and any other people he comes into contact with. Children who are articulate are much better able to control their behaviour and have no need to resort to aggression because they do not suffer from the frustration of bottled up emotions.

When children associate pleasure with books it gives them a *motive to learn to read*. Knowing that books tell exciting and interesting stories will make them more prepared to accept the tasks they have to do in learning to read, and they will be willing to make a greater effort.

By five, children will be taking a more active part in reading. Through the repeated hearing of favourite books, the child will recite stories from memory as though he was reading the printed page. By seven some children are fair readers and enjoy reading what they can for themselves. This does not mean that the adult no longer needs to read to the child, on the contrary, contribution at this stage is vital. The adult can read books which have complex ideas and language which the child could not tackle himself but which will develop his thinking and imagination.

Children, as indeed we all do, struggle with ethical concepts:

Why it is wrong to steal
Why should we help each other
Why it can be dangerous to talk to strangers
Why should we be forgiving, etc.

Bible stories, Greek myths, Fairy stories, all assist adults to help children to understand those questions and many others. *They serve to reinforce the moral teaching the child is getting at home and at school.*

Introduced to a large choice of books, *children will learn to differentiate between what is fact and what is fiction.* New interests are being constantly stimulated by such activities as a visit to a castle or a zoo, a programme on television about wild life or the Eskimos, for instance, can trigger off some special interest, and children will devour *books which give them information.* One week it may be books about snakes which hold the greatest attraction, the next week it may be aeroplanes or a book on Tudor kings and queens, butterflies, the planets or coal mines; the list is endless. Books which reflect their current passion give children enormous satisfaction. These can be taken out of the library or bought for the child, and what an opportunity provided for learning! It never ceases to amaze me that however complicated and technical the vocabulary, a child will remember if it refers to a subject he is interested in. A child who enjoys books need never know what it is to be bored! Books expose their minds to new ideas and give a love of learning.

To have plenty of books in the house is one of the wisest investments parents can make and joining a library with their child is another!

Why read to children   Have you understood?
1   Make a list of the things that the author says books can do for children.
2   Make a list of the times when it is particularly helpful to read to a child.
3   Under the heading 'When to read to a child' several examples are given of how reading can help a child. Write them down in your own words.

When to read to children

The answer to that is of course – anytime when the adult and child can sit and share a story together. Reading to a child is the most comforting and intimate experience: the child sits on the knee or certainly very close to the reading adult and can participate by turning pages, making comments about the pictures, joining in when familiar phrases or rhymes occur; 'I'll huff and I'll puff and I'll blow your house down,' to quote an old favourite.

Making 'reading a story' part of the *bedtime ritual* makes bedtime something to be looked forward to and helps the child face the fear and loneliness of separation from his beloved adults at the end of the day. It is also a good way *to make a child relax* in quiet contentment during the bustle, hustle and noise of everyday life. It is a soothing activity which can *help a child recover from an upset*, be it a tantrum, or a fall. It helps to avoid boredom during a wait in a doctor's surgery, the airport, a long car journey or just on a rainy afternoon. *When children are unwell* they find it very comforting to be read to. At such times old favourites are particularly reassuring.

Reading a story is also a good way of *making a relationship* with a child when babysitting. It can also be a way of making a visiting child feel welcome. One mother always read to her small daughter when she was breast feeding the baby: all three enjoying it.

What to read to children

Books
0–6 months – *Single pictures and talkabouts*
picture books – their surroundings
mobiles – catalogues
nursery rhymes

6 months–2½ years – Simplicity
Ladybird 'talkabout' books
Dick Bruna books and MacDonald 345
Rhymes – finger rhymes
Simple stories, eg *Hungry Caterpillar*

2½ years–4 years – Facts
Rhymes – in stories (Ladybird books) A.A. Milne
Stories – children, animals, TV characters
Classics – *House at Pooh Corner*, Beatrix Potter, Train Books
Factual 'Althea' books
Richard Scarry books
Books and themes, eg lighthouses, trains

4–5 years – *Imagination*
Fairy stories
Magic – Meg and Mog books
Humour – Mr Gumpy, Don't forget the bacon, Lear nonsense rhymes

General
Music – Number songs and rhymes
Pop-up books – Ricky and Chuckles, Ian Pienkowski
Number books

Other points
Difference between reading stories and telling stories: telling stories can

involve your own children directly tailor made for them, often quite
satisfied with re-telling of day's events in story form.

When reading or telling stories, voice intonation can make or break the
spell. Young children don't notice how good an accent or whatever is but
they do get bored with a droning voice.

Books for younger age can be used with older children when they're not
feeling well, or when starting to read themselves. Often like 'reading' the
books to younger brothers or sisters.

Can tape record your own stories on to own tapes to play any time –
don't have to buy prerecorded expensive tapes.

Don't forget the Library – very good selection.

What the first child likes isn't necessarily what the second or third may
like and vice versa – the child dictates what it likes – if he or she is
interested, he or she will show it.

Danger of frightening children? or using books to cyrstalise and control
their innate fears.

Books used
o–6 months
Mothercare catalogue
Ladybird Picture Books
Animal board book
Transport 'plastic paper' book (Purnell)
'Concertina' photograph book (Blackie)
'In a house I know' Leila Berg and John Walmsley (a Methuen
  chatterbook)
Ladybird nursery rhymes
Picture Lion nursery rhymes

6–18 months
Ladybird 'Talkabout' books
Ladybird 'Telling the Time'
Ladybird 'Finger Rhymes'
Ladybird 'Bedtime Rhymes'
'One to Ten and Down Again' (Mothercare/Readers Digest)

Toddler stage
Mr Men books
TV books, eg Pigeon Street
Dick Bruna books, eg Miffy
Railway Engine books Rev T. Awdry
'Hanibal the Hamster' – Ladybird series
'Action' books:
Pop up series (Intervisual Communications) Early Learning Centre
Child's Play action books (also ELC)
Hungry Caterpillar
Where is the Green Parrot?

On the Farm (Child's Play moments) Child's Play International.
When we were very young and The House at Pooh Corner, A.A. Milne

Playgroup age
Picture Lion books, eg Helpers, Mog
Althea Dinosaur books, eg Going to Dentist
Emma and Thomas books – Gunilla Wolde

Pre-school age
Mrs Pepperpot's Busy Day and Don't Forget the Bacon, Alf Proysen
  Picture Puffins
Meg and Mog books
My Naughty Little Sister
Richard Scarry books
Compendiums of fairy stories.

EXAMPLE

Julie recalls taking her sister Sammy down to the library:

Library
This is one place that Sammy loves to go to, because she loves books. I took Sammy down to the library and got her a ticket. Samantha was really excited about being able to get four books out, all of her own choice. When I went into the adult library Sammy kept on saying to me that she wanted to go to the children's library.

When we did go to the children's library Sammy wanted me to read her some stories. I read her a couple, and then she picked up a couple of books. She went for the ones that were colourful, and only had a small amount of writing on each page. Samantha loves simple drawings, and this is why she likes Miffy books.

Another reason why Sammy loves going to the library is that there is always a lot of other children there. Sammy always gets talking to them, and makes friends with them. Samantha also likes the library because there is always other things to do there. Such as the Old Clothes and weapons. There are a couple of skulls and Sammy really loves to go and see these. Also the old caves and cavemen and women.

If a book is overdue Sam does not like taking it back late because she always thinks that she is going to get told off for it being late.

Apart from that Sam really loves going to the library.

WORK GUIDE TO CHILDREN'S BOOKS

1 **Read** 15 to 20 children's stories.
Record Title-author of book

What insight into children did the story give you?

What moral and teaching point did it convey?

When you have completed reading this random sample of children's books:

2 Select six for detailed study: guide provided (below)

3 Read the examples of children's stories printed in this section of the book written by students.

A Brother for Luke is a story which prepares a child for a new experience, in this case the birth of a baby brother. Notice how the author has put herself into the world of the child and writes the story from his viewpoint, that illustrations reflect this as well.

The second story gives an insight into how the child from the best intentions, but because of his limited experience, sets out to please his parents, but her efforts end in chaos. Notice how understanding adults need to be on these occasions to grasp the child's motive and not to blame them for the result!

4 Write your own story for a child and make it into a book.

Scrap books, small photograph albums or even corn flake packets make useful book material.

For your *central character* use a *real person* – either yourself when little or a child you actually know. This will make your story much easier to write as you will know how the child feels and looks and reacts.

If you choose to write a story which prepares the child for a new experience make sure you prepare the child for the role he is going to play and describe what will be expected of him by others eg the dentist – to lie back; look in the mirror; spit in a bowl etc. and don't forget to describe the sound the drill makes!

Be aware of special or unfamiliar words eg stethoscope, injection, bandage. Remember all words are new to children so don't feel you need to use just 'simple' words. Children are very observant of detail in pictures, so give real thought to your illustrations. If you find drawing difficult use collage, a technique of making up a picture from magazine cut outs, coloured paper, bits of fabric etc; or get someone else to illustrate your story – if the child you are writing for is over four years, he will be able to do it!

5 Visit a children's library:

Prepare a questionnaire before you go that you can ask the librarian.

Notice books on display.

Find out activities for children that the Library provides.

Take the child with if you can.

Work guide to children's books

Study six children's stories – three must be longer, eg

Jacob Two Two

The Owl Who Was Afraid of The Dark
One which takes the children into other worlds, eg
Fairy Tales
One about every day events and things, eg
What Do People Do All Day
R. Scarry
Story with characters they can identify with, eg
Little Pete Stories
My Naughty Little Sister
An Anteater Named Arthur
A stort which helps a child come to terms with a trauma – anxiety or cope with strong feelings, eg
Just Awful
Where The Wild Things Are
A Baby Sister For Frances
Choose two – if possible one of your own childhood favourites.

WORKSHEET

Guide to reviewing children's books

1   Give title, author and describe appearance of the book, eg the size, the illustrations, etc.

2   Suggest the age of the child who would enjoy the book and describe the type of child to whom the book would appeal.

3   Give an outline of the story and pick out any interesting incidents, eg a sad bit or a funny bit, and say why incidents made an impression on you.

4   Describe the main character/s and say whether you think the child will be able to identify with the characters.

5   If there is a moral or teaching point to the story, say what it is.

6   Suggest ways in which the illustrations help in the story telling: draw an example.

7   What talking points will the story provide for the child and adult.

8   Give your personal reaction to the story – what insight into children did I get from it – and say if you think you will buy it for your own child.

9   If you have personal experience of the book, eg it was a story that you had read to you when you were a child or if you have read it to a child – describe the reactions.

EXAMPLES

A LITTLE BROTHER FOR LUKE

A story written (and illustrated) by Lorraine Cade to help prepare a child for a new experience: the birth of a baby brother. When reading this story notice the student's ability not only to *feel* the experience from the child's point of view but to *see* it like that as well.

One day Luke was getting ready to sit on his mother's lap for a story that his mother would tell him every afternoon at about this time. Sometimes it was the three little bears. He liked this because there was a lot of growling in it, and other times it was the hungry caterpillar.

Luke got all his books together and said to his mother excitedly, 'What book shall we have today then?'

'Well, I was thinking I'll make one up today' his mother told him.

'Oh Goody! I love it when you make them up' shouted Luke excitedly.

'Well the story is about a little boy called Luke.'

'That's my name', shouted Luke again.

'Well' his mother said 'That little boy is a bit different his Mummy has just had a baby boy a little brother for Luke. Well Luke loved this baby he played with it. Before he didn't have any one to play with and he wanted to share all his toys with someone. As the baby grew up they used to play together in the park with the sand, on the swings and the slide, chasing one another around the house and playing football in the garden, and life was really fun for them.

They shared everything even clothes. Toys that Luke's little brother had he shared with Luke. They even shared secrets together. They also made up stories about being space men.

The real Luke cried out excitedly 'Mummy, Mummy, I want a little brother like that, can we save up and buy one, please Mummy'.

'You see Luke I've got a surprise for you, very soon now I have to go into hospital', his mother replied.

'Have you fallen over and cut your knee like I did yesterday?' Luke jumped off his mother's lap and slightly lifted up her skirt and looked at her knees.

'They seem allright. What's wrong with you then mummy?'

'You don't always go to hospital because you're sick or cut yourself. In fact, you know you wanted to buy a baby, well you don't buy babies at all, they come out of Mummies' tummys and they are born in hospitals. You see maybe very soon now you are going to have a baby brother or a sister.'

'I don't want a sister', Luke cried out.

'You can have just as much fun with a sister', his mother replied

'Are you sure?' asked Luke.

'Yes of course, look how much fun James has with his sister Mary.'

Luke got very excited he couldn't stop talking about the fact that he was going to have a baby brother or a sister.

The next morning they went into the baby shop to buy some nappies for the baby and some new trousers for Luke.

'Why don't you and Daddy save up buy the baby a toy and you can start to play with him when you visit us in hospital, but you won't be able to play with the baby too much at the beginning because he is a little bit too small but later you can.'

A few weeks later Luke got up as usual for his breakfast but Mummy wasn't making the breakfast. Daddy was. 'Where's mummy?' Luke asked. His father told him 'she's gone to the hospital Luke, she had to be rushed there last night, I stayed up the hospital most of the night, and the nextdoor neighbour babysat for me to look after you in case you woke up'.

'When is she going to have the baby?' Luke asked.

'She has had it, it's a boy'. His father told him.

'A boy, oh goody! Hurrah!', Luke said jumping up and down until he was worn out.

'Hurry up and have your breakfast and we will go out to the shops and buy Mummy a card and the baby a toy then we will visit her in hospital', Daddy told Luke.

'I've never been to a hospital before', Luke said.

Luke was really excited that he ate his breakfast really fast. Then daddy and Luke went in to his bedroom and got dressed. Daddy helped Luke because he couldn't get dressed by himself yet. Luke couldn't stop talking about it he was so excited.

When they got to the shops they looked around at all the lovely toys and they both decided to get a lovable cuddly bear with a light blue ribbon. Luke told his father 'He looks like the baby bear in my book, *The Three Bears*'.

'Oh yes, so he does', his father said. Daddy also brought Luke a little wooden truck. They went into a newsagents and looked at the cards. They couldn't decide which one to get there were lots of them which were for new brothers and sisters. They were all pink and blue. But then eventually they chose one that was nearly as big as Luke it was huge.

They had tons of bags to carry. Luke couldn't hardly see where he was going. They struggled to the car and drove off to the hospital. Luke was jumping up and down on the back seat then they stopped and parked in a car park and there were millions of other cars there.

'Isn't it big' shouted Luke when they were in the hospital.

'Shhhh, people are in bed', Daddy whispered.

'At dinnertime?', whispered Luke.

'Yes, they aren't very well', Daddy told him.

'Oh!' Luke whispered again.

They walked a long way and they stopped outside a room with a big window, Daddy put all the presents down then picked Luke up and inside there was lots of plastic boxes with holes in the sides and tops were see-through and you could see lots of little babies some were asleep and others were crying and others were just laying there staring around the room.

'Where's my brother?', Luke asked.

'He's with mummy so that we can see him', Daddy said.

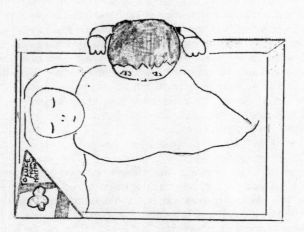

Daddy put Luke down and picked up the presents they went through a door and inside there were lots of beds with Mummies in them. Most of them had babies in their arms and others had them in a box like there was in the room with the big window but these boxes didn't have a lid.

Luke heard his name being called he looked around and saw his Mummy he ran over and his mother patted the bed as if to say 'jump up', he scrambled on the bed and sat by his mother. His father gave his wife the card and the present.

'Where's my brother?' asked Luke.

'He's over there', his mother pointed to the box. Luke jumped down off the bed and took the teddy bear to play with his brothers and inside the box there was a tiny baby, and also by the baby was a present all wrapped up and on the box the words were 'To Luke From Matthew'.

'Is his name Matthew then?' said Luke pleased.

His mother smiled and nodding, 'yes Luke'.

'Oh, thank you Matthew!' Luke said. He opened his present and it was a small box of Lego to make a car with.

After an hour Daddy said, 'Come on we will have to go home now and have dinner and then we will come back tomorrow'.

'Oh I don't want to go now', Luke said stubbornly.

'Come on Luke, don't be naughty now you've been so good', Daddy said nearly getting cross.

'Oh all right'. Luke kissed his Mummy and brother then they went home. When they got home Luke helped his Daddy to cook the dinner, it was hard work.

The next day they saw Luke's mother and brother again and also nanny came to stay and she brought everyone presents.

Father told Luke, 'Mummy is coming home tomorrow and she is going to bring Matthew home'.

'Brilliant! then I can play football with him', Luke shouted.

'No', his dad laughed 'not yet when he starts to walk you can, son'.

'Oh all right daddy, I'll wait.'

The next day came fast and Daddy and Luke made all the beds even the cot that used to be Luke's for Matthew to sleep in. Nanny had to fetch Mummy from the hospital.

They were in the middle of dusting when the door bell rang. Luke ran to the door, he stood on tiptoe and opened the door and there was Mummy with his brother Matthew in her arms and Nanny standing there.

'Welcome home', shouted Luke and Daddy at the same time and laughed and everyone was happy.

THE END

GOOD INTENTIONS

Once upon a time there was a naughty little girl called Celia who was five years old. She was chubby and bouncy and was continually getting into trouble, sometimes without meaning to. She had light brown hair and big, dark brown eyes. She had a little up-turned nose and a small mouth. She was full of life and when she couldn't get her own way she would scream and shout and throw a tantrum. She was quite clever and she adored music of all kinds. She would sing and dance to any kind of music. She loved to fight and play with children of her own age. She loved babies and small animals as well. She was very lovable and everybody liked her. She had a lot of friends too.

One day she thought she would help her parents by spring-cleaning the house for them. She got up early one sunny morning before her parents were up and thought she would begin by spring-cleaning the kitchen. She thought what a lovely surprise it would be for them to wake up and find the house spic and span! That would make her parents love her even more and they would tell everybody what a lovely, helpful little girl she was. She might even get a new toy or a game as a reward. Or perhaps a big box of sweets!

With this happy thought in mind she started to clean the kitchen. She put on her Mummy's apron which was far too big for her, and got out the mop and bucket from a cupboard. She remembered the last time she tried to clean the kitchen. Her parents were in the front room watching television at the time. They heard the noise she was making and came in. She was spanked and sent to bed without any supper. And all because she wanted to help! This time she vowed she would make a success of the spring-cleaning. She would not make any noise at all in case it woke them up.

She then started to pull out all the crockery from the cupboards, and then she got out a bucket of water and started to wash out the cupboards with a mop. Then she filled the sink with water, went over to the vegetable rack and took a pound of potatoes from it, took them over to the sink and put them in the water. She left behind a trail of earth along the kitchen floor.

Then she got the washing-up liquid and squirted it all over the kitchen floor. Then she got the mop and rubbed the washing-up liquid into the floor to make it nice and shiny. It was also very shiny and difficult to walk on. Then, still holding the mop, she dipped in the bucket of water and started to wash the walls and ceiling. Soon the whole ceiling was dripping wet, but Celia just carried on regardless. She was determined to spring-clean the whole house from top to bottom before her parents woke up.

When she finished washing down the walls and ceiling she stepped back to admire her work and skidded on the slippery floor. She fell and cried out and knocked over the food-rack. It fell with a crash, spilling all its contents over the floor. Carrots, sprouts, cabbages and potatoes all tumbled out and mixed together. Celia was very angry because of this, but she calmed herself down and started to get the breakfast ready. She got the milk from the fridge and carefully carried it over to the table. But unlucky for Celia the milk bottle was wet and slippery and she dropped it when she reached the table. It smashed all over the table and glass and milk went flying in all directions. Celia went stiff with alarm and fear. Surely her parents would have heard the noise! She glanced quickly round the kitchen. What a mess! There was earth and water all over the floor, and piles of crockery and food were dripping wet ánd tumbled in confusion all over the floor. The vegetable rack was on its side, all the cupboard doors were open and water dripped off the walls and ceiling in torrents. The sink was filled with potatoes, and the kitchen table was covered in milk and broken glass.

If her parents came in and saw this mess they'd have a fit. In despair she started to cry. She'd been so looking forward to all the presents and praise she'd get if she cleaned the house for Mummy and Daddy. Now she wouldn't get anything except a telling off and a hiding. As she had expected Celia's parents did come in the kitchen to see what all the noise was about.

'Celia, what on earth was all that noise?' said Mummy, angrily looking at the mess in the kitchen. 'What have you been doing?'

Mummy and Daddy looked very cross indeed, and Celia was afraid of what they might do to her. She sobbed even louder and said, 'Please don't be cross with me. I didn't mean to do it, I was only trying to help. I was going to spring-clean the house for you so you'd be pleased. But then everything went horribly wrong and you woke up!'

Surprisingly Mummy and Daddy weren't so angry with her this time as they were last time, because they realized that Celia was only trying to help. They first gave her a telling off and a lecture and Celia helped them to clean up the mess she had made. She promised she would never do that again. She didn't get a new toy, or a game, or a box of sweets as she has planned for, and she didn't get a punishment either, as she had expected. She felt very relieved and happy and she promised she would never do anything without her parents' permission first, otherwise it could go horribly wrong.

Celia grew into a happy, bouncy girl, and although she did many more naughty things she never again tried to spring clean the house.

THE END

Babysitting: Getting used to the babysitter

A babysitter, whether a day-time sitter to enable the mother to shop or go to the hairdresser, or an evening sitter to enable the parents to go out socially, becomes a significant person in the child's life as a bridge between home and the outside world.

Before the babysitter takes on this responsibility, he or she should have made preliminary visits to the home in order to make a relationship, become familiar with the layout of the house and the child's way of communicating, including rituals such as going to bed or to the toilet. It is essential for the parents to leave an emergency 'phone number at all times.

The aim is to make the child look forward to the babysitter's arrival rather than become anxious because the parents are leaving. The babysitter should be prepared to read stories and play games with the child.

The basic responsibilities, tasks and problems for a babysitter can be summaried as follows:

Reasons why asked to babysit
For parents to have a bit of freedom from their children
To enable the mother to go shopping or to the hairdresser
For parents to go out together for a meal, or a social evening
Because of a sudden emergency.
Because the mother may go out to work regularly.

Responsibilities
Safety – you have to keep an eye on the child and make sure he is safe.
Form a relationship – you have to form some sort of relationship with the child or he will always be crying for his mum.
Occupy the child – you have to keep the child occupied or he will get bored.
Personal involvement – get involved with him/her.

Tasks
Prepare the child for bed.
To feed, change and dress him.
Wash him.
To cook a meal for him.
To do household chores.
Play and watch television with him.

Problems

Will not do as he is told.

Keeps coming down when put to bed.

Refuses to eat.

May be naughty – disobedient, aggressive or destructive.

Make a fuss about how you handle him.

May be unhappy or missing his parents.

Illness and accidents may occur.

He may have had bad dreams or something has frightened him.

Child may feel insecure with babysitter.

He may be 'trying you out'.

He may be seeing 'how far' he can go.

Solutions

Make a relationship with child before you babysit.

Approach a child gently and slowly.

Play with him.

Always be efficient.

Think ahead – plan – be prepared.

Explain your ways (rules) be consistent.

The child needs your personal involvement and interest.

Forming relationships

You need to know the child and he needs to know you. Play it cool meeting children. Observe what kind of child they are and try to understand them.

The provision of 'Childspace'

As a society we are remiss in our provision of childspace in public places and indeed there is no emphasis on the needs of the child at all. No wonder that adults with children using such places sometimes expect the wrong thing from them and the child is regarded as naughty – when the situation gives the child little alternative.

For instance, in a shoe shop, shoes for children are usually up or downstairs, making it difficult for the parent and making an upset more likely; supermarkets do not provide toilet facilities and very often display tempting goods, such as sweets, within children's reach. As members of the community we should become more aware of the effect of these problems on the development of the child and the opportunities lost.

The idea that children should be seen and not heard needs re-examination – sometimes it is appropriate, sometimes it is not.

Changing work patterns suggest that workplaces must increasingly consider crêches as essential. Also – would more people attend religious services if special account were taken of children's needs? It is these and other lack of provisions that further limit not only the experience and progress of the child – but also the relationship between child and parent.

PART III

Seeing the World from the Child's View Point

Dana's funny story
I was sitting with my daughter Dana, who was
two and a half, in a very quiet surgery – where
no one speaks.

Well, Dana, very talkative, like many of her
age, chose that moment to pass wind.

You can imagine that was embarrassing
enough, but after a moment she turned to me and
said – 'Sorry mummy my bum burped', which I
and quite a few patients could not suppress
laughing.

Guide to using Part III

This is most important section of the book.

1 It concentrates on **play** which demonstrates how children learn about the properties of materials, competence, and the way people behave to each other.

2 It focuses on understanding children's **behaviour** and supplies questions to test the understanding of the content.

The content of both subjects is complex but coming to grips with each section is facilitated by the use of the three components of the course:

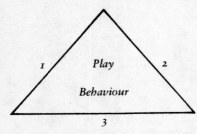

1   Learning the body of knowledge
2   Observation of children
3   Recall of own experience of childhood

Observation of children can happen anywhere, eg in the street, on the bus, in the supermarket, at the cinema. In the classroom, playgroup sessions can *focus* on the subjects studied. *Parents of children are a most valuable source of examples and information.*

Students' own recollection of childhood both at play and when unravelling the complexities and quirks of behaviour supply the most important links. Recorded in this section are examples of students' writing which could help others identify their own similar experiences when they were children.

Play section

The work can be approached in a variety of ways. There is a comprehensive guide to a research project at the end of the section. I suggest the section requiring pupils to write about their play experiences under the six categories suggested should be undertaken while the section on play is being studied. There are several examples written by students which show how the subject could be approached.

Designing playing spaces could also be done simultaneously. Reading the whole section at one sitting could prove a daunting task.

Understanding behaviour

Before undertaking the study of this concentrated look at behaviour, I suggest *the work sheet on Mischief is completed* by students first. The examples they record can be compared to the ones supplied by students in the book.

When the study of the section is complete *the analytical work sheet on behaviour can be undertaken*. It is constructed in a more formal way to allow students to demonstrate their acquired knowledge and understanding. Examples written by students in this section are also supplied – they show fascinating insights into what motivated them in their childhood to behave the way they did.

Play

Why children play

Play is the core of a child's development in the world. A recently born child is new to the world and the world is new to him. As play begins, the child learns:

About himself or herself
About other people
About the world and how it works.

As adults we know what happens when we throw a pebble into the water. We can predict that if a container has a hole in the bottom, it will not hold water. We know why. But we didn't always have this knowledge. We learned, as all young children learn, by the experiences and experiments that we call *play*.

Play can take up all of the child's attention for there is so much to explore in the world, such as:

Shape (round, square)
Texture (rough, smooth, slippery)
Consistency (hard, soft)
Colour
Taste.

We know all children do not develop at the same rate, but there is a pattern of development which is common to normal children.

In the same way children of different ages reach different 'play stages', and progress through these stages is a matter of maturity. For example here are three stages of pretend play:

1 A one year old child will imitate actions that go with nursery rhymes and will play pee-po.

2 By two years old a child will devote much time to pretend play, the theme of which will be centred on household chores and other everyday experiences of real life.

3 But from three years onward, the child's pretend play becomes more complex and much of it is based on fantasy from stories the child hears and the programmes watched on television. Not only will the content of the child's play be more complex but the child will begin being involved in playing co-operatively with other children.

A knowledge of the average ages at which a child masters certain skills will help the adult to know what to expect and be able to provide play opportunities which will help the child on to the next stage of development.

Although children learn best if they are allowed to go on at their own pace, *they need adults.*

A young child needs to play near his mother. He will not be able to concentrate unless the 'security figure' is in sight.

Children need adults to help them when they have not mastered a particular skill – like threading a needle. They become frustrated and cannot carry on with the activity unless they receive help from the adult.

Children sometimes do not have the strength to do something they wish to do, such as carrying a bucket full or water to the sand pit. Patient willingness on the part of the adult to be at hand and help them, even if it means interrupting the daily routine, will indirectly teach the child to grow into a helpful person.

Learning to share and take turns needs adult example and intervention before it can be achieved. At two a child is very likely to snatch a spade from another child. The adult is needed to show 'calm' disapproval and to find a solution to the dilemma. It is essential that two children should not be left to fight it out.

Children are often not aware of safety hazards and require adult supervision. A friend of mine looked up from her washing to see the group of four to seven year olds, who were playing in the garden on the climbing frame, put a rope around another child's neck. Then the command was given to 'jump'! Luckily intervention was hastily made and the child was rescued.

As adults we must be aware of the importance and significance of children's play and it is our job to:

Provide play space (in, and where possible, out of doors)
Organise the play materials
Allow opportunities for messy play
Join in – chasing, throwing a ball, playing board games, etc.
Make opportunities for children to be together so they can play.

We are there to extend the child's knowledge to encourage and praise him when a new skill is acquired. In this way we give the child confidence to make further attempts because the new skill is now known to be of value. It is also our role as adults to explain new techniques and always be ready with kisses and cuddles when things go wrong.

What have you learned?   Why children play
1   Pick out the two words that tell you what play is.
2   You are told that the child learns about himself – what two other large areas of learning are mentioned?
3   What five qualities does the child learn about?
4   Explain in your own words the meanings of: Pattern of development; Maturity.
5   Five reasons are given why children need aaults as they play. What are they?
6   State the nine tasks for adults to do with children's play.

7　Look up the word *category* and make sure you understand it.

8　Write down the six categories of play activities.

9　Give three reasons why children need physical play.

10　Give three reasons why children have accidents.

11　Explain the meaning of regress.

12　Study the section on pretend play and then without looking at the book write down as many reasons as you can why such play is important.

13　What sort of experiences help a child develop their drawing?

14　Where is the earliest place for a child to draw?

16　The first thing a child enjoys with paint is seeing colour appear. What are the next stages?

With what children play

Choosing toys should depend on some knowledge and understanding of a child's development, the stage reached, planning for the next stage, and regard for safety.

Toys are expensive but as they are aids to the child's development they should be chosen with care and the purchase of 'key' toys should be planned.

Providing suitable tools for play means the child finds satisfaction in what he is doing, stops him from being bored and frustrated and offers channels for learning.

Toys children play with: a guide to good toys

All children need a soft toy. A favourite one becomes their constant companion. So when shopping remember the toy needs to be strong, have a good face, and eyes that are not easily removed or destroyed. Avoid flashy soft toys of the kind that have satin paws, etc – they are not going to last!

With dolls and teddy bears, the child acts out events that have happened during the day. When playing with dolls and other soft toys, the child is in control and the toys are made to take on any role that is required.

The favourite soft toy is not only a comforter in times of trouble and a secure presence to snuggle down to sleep with or visit unfamiliar people or places with but *it is often made to act as a go between* the child and the adult. There are situations when the child either doesn't want to admit to something because of an obviously unfavourable response or is uncertain of the response and therefore tests it out using a teddy or a doll as a self-substitute. There are other situtations when the child is ashamed of something and uses teddy as a culprit, eg 'Mummy, Teddy's afraid to go to sleep'. ('I'm not, I'm a big girl').

Bricks

Around 35 are needed for satisfying buildings to grow. Pillars and arching bricks aid to the possibilities and extend the child's imagination. It is better to buy plain unpainted wooden bricks because these give the illusion of reality. They do not need to be bought all at once but can be collected over several years. A large laundry basket full of bricks will provide endless play possibilities. They are a much better buy than a garage, fort or even a doll's house, *because the child can create buildings and alter those to fit any design or purpose.*

A mobility toy
From about 18 months onwards children gain considerable satisfaction from a toy that they can make move. A start can be made by pushing a small trolley and then graduating to a small wooden bicycle without pedals. The child can push this, eventually graduating to a tricycle. All these can be bought second hand.

Points to look out for are:
Thick wheels
Heavy pedal bars that won't bend with the crashes
Rubber pedals, *not* breakable plastic ones
Metal seats also break, so look for a vinyl one with vinyl seat.

Children love their bicycles to be bright colours – and usually red is the most popular. Accessories can be added, like a rope for towing wagons, a bell, a licence plate and a basket. If the child does not have a garden in which to enjoy riding around, regular outings to the park with the bike are very important.

Do It Yourself toys
Tree Houses are magical but not all children are able to have one. But it is quite easy to make a house or a space ship. A shop has great play appeal and it can be made from a large cardboard box. These large cardboard boxes can also make play houses.

With a sharp knife doors can be cut out, as well as windows or peepholes. Children can decorate the inside and outside with crayons and paint. They can also paste on pictures from magazines and bright pieces of fabric or even use up oddments of wallpaper. Carpet ends can be placed on the floor and furniture can be made out of cardboard. Also these play houses can always be discarded when necessary and a new one created without cost – but with a good deal of fun.

Presents that are not toys
All children love to use tools that make things happen, such as a hole puncher, a stapler, a labelling gun, an egg timer, a whisk – or a strainer.

A collection of household items for play
From toddler stage, children are most interested and curious about real objects, such as the telephone, the turntable on a record player, the saucepans being used in the kitchen. After the age of two, they begin to accept toys which are symbols of the real world. It is a good idea to keep a box in the kitchen cupboard with 'real' items for the child to play with, such as a tin pie dish, an

old saucepan, a plastic freezer container, plastic bottles, an old telephone. Jumble sales can provide excellent sources for this sort of collection.

A junk box
Every playgroup and primary school has a store of cardboard boxes, egg boxes, yogurt cartons, toilet rolls, milk bottle tops, old wallpaper rolls. Together with strong glue, glue brushes and scissors *with round edges* great fun can be had. When observing children using these junk materials it soon becomes obvious from their absorption how much satisfaction and enjoyment they get from making things from assorted junk materials.

Scrapbooks
I have seen toddlers sitting happily on a potty looking at a scrapbook in which birthday cards have been stuck. Scrapbooks are very easy to complete and they can reflect a current interest inspired by a visit to a zoo, or another interesting place the child has visited. Older children will take much pleasure in looking back at these, and also will enjoy making their own. The may also decide to keep an illustrated diary or start to collect stamps or Victorian postcards. Whatever the outcome, a scrapbook is a quiet activity which can give much satisfaction and is a very good introduction to the kind of project work children are required to do at school.

Music
Young children will enjoy listening to nursery rhymes, whilst older ones will take pleasure from listening to a record of *Peter and the Wolf* or some other story.

Remember – Toys are for doing – not having!

Storing toys
Storing toys needs as much care and planning as arranging the kitchen – and should have priority consideration in any house which has children.

Open shelves at a child level are best. These can be arranged and rearranged as required. The different toys can be placed on these in anything from labelled shoe boxes to plastic ice cream containers.

Vegetable racks also make excellent toy storage. *Egg boxes* are very useful for putting away tiny things, eg Action man accessories. *It is also important to have some cupboard space which is out of reach where special toys can be put away.*

Laundry baskets, cane or plastic are excellent in which to keep bricks or toddler toys. *Nylon net bags hang on hooks* and can have items put away in them such as sand or water toys. *Self adhesive cork panels* are useful and children can display pictures on them – or birthday cards.

Efficient storage of toys avoids unnecessary breakages, makes it much easier to clean up, helps in training children in good order habits and ensures that their property is treated with respect and care. This will quickly teach children to respect adult's property both at home, when visiting or when they begin school.

What have I learned?   With what children play

1   What must you bear in mind when choosing a toy for a child?
2   What are the most important things to look for in a soft toy?
3   How does the child use the soft toy?
4   What is the advantage in buying bricks rather than a fort or doll's house?
5   What should you look for when buying a bicycle or tricycle?
6   How do you make cardboard boxes into playhouses?
7   Can you think of any item from a household shop or department which children would enjoy using but which are not mentioned?
8   What other 'real items' can you think of that a child might enjoy playing with from the age of two?
9   List the quiet attitudes mentioned under the heading 'Scrap Books'.
10   Draw a sketch of a room showing storage features suggested and label these features.
11   Describe the characteristic ways the following ages play with others:
Two year old
Three year old
Five year old.

Children's play activities
Children's play activities can be separated into six categories:

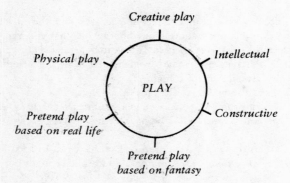

When observing children at play you will often see several of these play categories combined at one time into a single activity. If you recall your own play, you will recognise how these different aspects of play come in together in one game. Take for example a game of Cowboys and Indians, which fits the category of 'pretend play based on fantasy'. When playing such a game you may also have painted your face or made an Indian head-dress which involved you in creative play. In addition some aspects of physical play would have also been invlolved as running and climbing were all part of the activity.

Normal play activities involve the body, mind and emotions, all of which develop as a wider variety of skills is required.

Learning to make friends
Social play
The learning of social play is a gradual process and passes through various stages. Learning to take turns, to share, to consider other people's feelings or needs and to follow rules demands complicated emotional adjustments. These can only be achieved by giving children plenty of opportunities to be together.

From birth until about 18 months, the child's play is centred on his own discoveries and experiments and the interaction of adults and much older children. But from about 18 months onwards children begin to derive satisfaction from playing alongside other children. This is called **parallel play** and will lead to the child becoming interested in other children's activities. At two, children only have a very few words and contact is established in physical ways, ie touching, loving, pulling, pinching, snatching toys. Children are continually experimenting. When observing this process it will become evident that when one child has pinched another who then bursts into tears, the experiment is repeated out of curiosity for the child is anxious to establish whether the other will *always* cry if pinched. Gradually children begin to co-operate in an activity for short periods of time, particularly in a simple task like building bricks together. *Because children in the early stages can only see matters from their own view point, they can only co-operate in an activity for short periods of time before becoming frustrated and needing adult intervention.*

Most three year olds who have had opportunities to go through these stages successfully, begin to want to join other children's games and are usually mature enough to understand that their acceptance depends on taking turns and sharing. They do now obey older children in a game, but they expect rules to be elastic and flexible, to be changed to suit themselves or will bend them to their own advantage. It is only between five and seven that children mature enough to recognise the need for mutually agreed rules.

As in all learning, children will sometimes regress in play. For example, if a four year old is unwell, the child will not be interested in group play. Also, when introduced to a new group the child may wish first to be an observer before deciding to join in.

Pretend play
As a toddler the child is an explorer discovering a small world. Then a scientist experimenting with its properties. Later the child becomes dominated by his imagination.

The pre-school child is usually being someone else and will try out every activity noticed about adults. The child will imitate their emotions as well as their actions, and in so doing reveal how he is spoken to and treated.

Children devise their own props if real ones are not available to them. A friend of mine would not allow her children war toys. As a result they would save toast from breakfast, chew it into the shape of a gun and then play the usual bang-bang games.

An adult can get inside a child's mind because they have been there before. But the child cannot get into an adult's mind. When a child plays at being a teacher, he or she is only interested in imitating the power the teacher has – not in imparting knowledge, ie marking, getting children to sit or stand or telling them off. In the same way when a child plays at being a doctor he is not interested in preventive medicine or medical science, but only with the doctor's powers of sticking needles into people, bandaging them up or listening to their chests with a stethoscope.

Sometimes the child will use pretend play to re-live incidents which were emotionally important, such as spending time in hospital. Being in hospital can be a very strange and terrifying experience for a child (and not just young children!), but when children play at hospitals in the comfort and security of home or school they can act out the things that frightened them and over which they had no control. By giving pretend injections to their toys or other children, the child gains control of the situation.

In remembering the most interesting parts of their experience in play, many children are better able to come to terms with their own fears. Often something a child is frightened of or is unsure about appears in their pretend play. Children act out stories which frighten them such as *Billy Goat Gruff* or stories about witches or ghosts, as well as the programmes they have watched on television. The *Dr Who* series has provided many such examples and school playgrounds were invaded by hosts of daleks.

In our imagination we can go anywhere, be anyone, do anything. It is important for children who usually have to do as they are asked. *In their pretend play it is they who can direct events.* When pretending to be a teacher, for instance, they can savour the feelings of being in authority or the shy, timid child can pretend to be really naughty.

In pretend play whether it is based on real life or fantasy, children take responsibility. It is they who drive buses, cook dinners and change the baby.

The way people behave towards each other is sometimes difficult for the child to understand. Why does Mummy keep talking to her friend and ignoring the child? Why do Mummy and Daddy get cross with each other? Why do they behave differently when visitors call or call granny an old cow? All this can be coped with better if the child is able to play it out.

Through pretend play the child can get rid of angry, destructive or even violent feelings. Teddy bears are buried in the sand, or the dolls have hell knocked out of them. In play the child can act out and so control any emotion and give love, hate or be tender or unforgiving.

Children reveal the way they feel about themselves in pretend play. The five year old pretending that he is a tiny kitten, really wants to be as small as his baby brother or sister. Like the baby he wants to be carried to bed in mother's arms.

Pretend play is also used by children as a means of escape from uncomfortable, humiliating or boring circumstances. Nicholas, aged four, was very jealous of his one year old brother who had just started to walk. He was being very difficult at home, and his mother took him to the doctor. While she was giving an account of his 'bad' deeds, Nicholas was performing an elaborate escape sequence whilst sitting on a chair.

A common occurence in childhood is the *invention of an imaginary friend* with whom the child will share conversations and activities. The child will expect the imaginary friend's likes and dislikes to be recognised and accommodated by the parents. Such inventions are quite common, particularly in only children. The invisible friend, usually with a well defined personality, acts as a substitute brother or sister.

A good deal of the child's pretend play involves copying how the adults about behave towards the child and towards each other. Their behaviour, tone of voice, mannerisms and language are accurately reproduced. *Television has also become a major influence and children copy what they see.*

Making a study of children's play is both a fascinating and a complex process. However, it is made a good deal easier for all of us because as children we have all experienced the aspects of play that we are learning about. I will now take each of the play categories in turn:

Physical play

Young children need to learn about themselves. They want to find out how to move quickly and safely, how to control what they do and how to master new movements and acquire co-ordination. Moving helps children judge distances and learn how hand and eye movements work together. They are learning this when they try to reach out for objects, or at a later stage when they try to catch a ball. Movement is also important for health – for bone and muscle must develop and grow. Children need exercise to do that.

Children have an amazing amount of energy and unless they are given ample opportunity for using up this energy, they become frustrated, bored and listless. Children must have space to move in, objects to climb on, crawl through and jump over. They must have opportunities to know what their bodies can do and what they can't do, for only through practice will they become confident and develop properly. Many aspects of physical play provide a child with a challenge and on meeting those challenges life becomes much more exciting.

Children do not attempt to do physical feats for which they do not feel ready. Adults who try to cajole children to climb higher, or go down a slide when the child is unwilling, are quite wrong. Children have an in-built safety valve – and only attempt activities if they are ready for them. But once they *are* ready, they will spend a good deal of time repeating the activity until they are completely confident in their mastery of it. Nervous adults try to stop children climbing to the top of the climbing frame or attempting other physically challenging feats.

But they should remember that children do not attempt to climb anything which they cannot manage, and if they do and find they have over stepped their ability – they invariably ask for help.

It is when the apparatus is faulty or the tree branch rotten, or the adult transfers his nervousness to the child or another child challenges them to undertake something they are not ready to do, that children have accidents. The adult's role is to check safety and supervise, allowing children to develop physical powers at their own pace and without interference. Children have accidents and hurt themselves when:

The apparatus is faulty or the tree branch they are climbing is rotten
The adult transfers his nervousness to the child, creating loss of confidence and concentration
A child dares another to do something for which he is not ready.

The adult should also always be ready to praise the child's achievements.

Creative play

Creative play means that the child makes something that did not exist before. It may be a clay model, a drawing, a painting, a brick building or a collage. On the other hand, the child is also being creative when splashing water, playing in sand or handling clay, because something is being made to happen. This gives the child experience of weight, volume, size and number. Also the adult can extend the value of this play even further by sharing with the child his new gift for words, so when playing in the sand vocabulary can be extended to include words such as dribble, scoop, mould, flatten, sift. New experiences will require new words and children often express ideas in the objects they make before they are able to find the right words.

All children are naturally creative and are very enthusiastic about making things. This means that through their creative play activities they learn *competence*, ie how to pour without spilling, how to control a paintbrush. These skills do not come to them all at once, but are acquired gradually through practise. Only if they enjoy their activities and find them fulfilling will they practise until skill is obtained.

The tools adults can supply will help the child play in different ways. When a child is playing with water, objects could be added for pouring, measuring, whisking and bubbling. Also objects that sink and float. The more imaginative these contributions are the more scope they can offer for creative play.

All play depends on the stage the child has reached, and this applies most particularly to drawing and painting.

Drawing

A child is ready to draw the moment a chubby wax crayon can be held. The child will soon begin to bang on the paper and will be surprised that marks are left behind. If magic markers are used as well as wax crayons, chalk and paint, the child will gradually scribble line drawings, until at around three years big head figures will be produced. Then, by seven years the child will be drawing a detailed and correctly proportioned human figure.

Drawings and painting help a child express feelings and record experiences, even when these may be too difficult to put into words. Looking at children's paintings and drawings will give clues as to what they find interesting and important. Psychologists and psychiatrists who help children who are emotionally disturbed, (whose feelings have been damaged in some way), can find out what is bothering a child by looking at his paintings and drawings. Quite often confusing or violent emotions can be controlled by expressing them in painting and drawing.

One small boy of four woke up regularly disturbed by fearful dreams of monsters. In desperation his mother suggested to him that he draw this monster. He did and he pinned his drawing above his bed. As a result the nightmares ceased. Another therapy for anger or anxiety can be manipulating messy substances like water, clay and paint.

Normally, a child starts by drawing people. Then gradually other shapes are added which represent houses, trees, cars, animals or anything else in the world. For the child's drawings to develop, stimulating experiences are needed. These experiences can be quite simple events such as a bus ride or a train journey, seeing workmen in the street, a window cleaner or walking on a windy day. All these activities provide material for a child's imagination – especially if the adult shares these experiences and talks about them.

Children draw what they *know* not what they *see*; a side view of a car will have all four wheels. They will emphasize what is *important* to them, which is why people always have large hands with lots of fingers – it is fingers that make things happen.

The easiest place for a child to draw at home is on the floor. Drawing paper is not a necessity for odds and ends of wall paper, old computer paper, lining wall paper, will do just as well. A clipboard with paper and pencil attached allows the child to draw whilst travelling in a car or on the train. A container with pencil crayons next to the bed with paper to draw on can occupy a child who is an early waker or be a soothing activity before sleep.

Painting

Not all children are going to be artists but they all need to learn about colour, texture and how to control a brush.

How children develop their painting: Very young children are not trying to paint pictures for they are more interested in experimenting with the paint. They enjoy sloshing with a paintbrush and seeing colour appear on the paper. Once they have exhausted their interest in this activity, many children go on to make more formal patterns. The next discovery is that paint will go on top of paint and paintings may become more decorative. Soon the child begins to paint people, houses, vehicles, animals and so on.

The object a child paints may not always be recognisable to an adult but they should always be treated with respect. The yellow blob is a giraffe seen at the zoo and fun should not be made of it. It is always a good idea to ask a child to explain what has been painted so the wrong guess can be avoided. This prevents shaking the child's confidence in what has been created.

In the first five years, a child learns more than at any other time. By encouraging exploration and self-expression, the adult is helping the child to develop a lively mind. By opening up opportunity, concentration is developed – an ability which is so important in all learning. Many of the creative activities that children find rewarding are very messy and require from the adult time in preparation or cleaning up. But they do pay high dividends. Sharing is all important for only through a real partnership between adult and child, can play lead to development.

Intellectual play

Board games

From about three years of age children are ready to join other people in playing games. There are many board and card games on the market, and all of them can help a child learn something about numbers, colours and words.

It is difficult for a child to learn to accept following rules. As they can only see things from their own point of view, they expect rules to be flexible to suit themselves and will become very frustrated if they do not. They need someone to play with them who is very patient and understands this. Playing regularly with such a person, the child will gradually master the difficult social skills of taking turns, following rules and learning to cope with losing.

It is tiring for young children to concentrate for long. Probably ten to fifteen minutes at a time is sufficient.

There are many games from which to choose. It is important to choose ones which are suitable for the age of the child. Pre-school children need very simple ones, with clear, brightly coloured pictures and a few simple rules.

EXAMPLES

Students' play recollections

Imaginative play based on fantasy
Cops and Robbers
Cowboys and Indians
Robots
Pirates

Title
The title of my imaginative play is *Pirates* and I was about six when I played it.

What happened in my game
We played pirates in the bedroom and we used to have all four mattresses on the floor and a sheet stretched across from one bunk bed to the other

and then we used to dare each other to walk the plank, which meant trying to walk across the sheet and if you didn't make it to the other side and you fell off you were eaten by the crocodiles on the floor. If you made it to the other side without falling off you were made the captain and then you could tell whoever you wanted to walk the plank and if they refused you could have them thrown in jail.

Who I involved in my game and what I used
In my game of Pirates it involved me Lorraine, Liza, Debbie and sometimes George. We used our beds and mattresses, sheets, pillows and blankets.

How I felt when playing it
When playing my Pirate game I felt proud whenever I reached the other side because I could then be in charge and I could tell my sisters what to do and if they never did it I would have the pleasure of throwing them in prison.

What I learned when playing it and what rules I had
I learnt from playing Pirates to take on a challenge and I also learnt what it is like to be in charge and to be boss. The rules are as follows. If you are dared to go across the sheet and you refuse you are thrown in prison and you stay there until someone else is thrown in and then you can come home. If you fall off you are eaten by the crocodiles and you have to lay still for ten minutes. If you reach the other side you can tell the others what to do.

Imaginative play based on real life
I was about four years old when I started to play this game.

What I did
In the game we used to play war. My brother is three years older than me so he used to play it on his own and then I joined in.

We used to have hundreds of little toy soldiers, half were green and half were beige. I used to have the beige.

We used to set all the soldiers up in the lounge; in the cabinets on the shelves, behind the ornaments, on the telly etc and then we positioned the last ones in rows ready for the battle. We also used to have little cannons that we filled with matchsticks (that had the ends cut off) so that we could 'kill' the other side. The cannons really worked, I remember pressing the little button and seeing the match fly out the end, it was great.

Where I played
We used to play this game mainly in the lounge, it used to take up the complete room and you could hardly walk through it for fear of treading on it all.

How I felt when playing it

When we played this game I used to feel so proud because of the way we had set it all up. I think I enjoyed the setting up of the game more than the actual playing, as it used to take hours to set it up and only about 15mins to destroy it all.

Adult involvement

My parents didn't really play the game with us, they sometimes helped us to set it up but I think me and my brother got more satisfaction from doing it ourselves.

They didn't mind us making a mess of the lounge and used to help us pack it all away at the end.

What learning value did it have

I think it taught me to play alongside other people, as I was at the age where I thought I could cheat to win, and it showed me that rules are for everyone including myself.

Intellectual play

When I first started to play board games I was about five years old.

Where we played

We mainly played them in the front room, usually on the table as the bits would get lost on the floor. Sometimes I played them in my bedroom or in my brother's room.

Who I involved

I usually played with my brother as he was very close to me. My sister was a bit older than me and was not interested. I loved my brother playing with me as he was always nice to me. But I think the best times were when everybody played: my Mum, my Dad, and my sister.

How I felt

When I just used to play with my brother I felt loved and that people were concerned about me. But the best times were when my Dad and family played, it seemed such a complete family and there seemed to be a glow around which squeezed us together. The main thing I remember is that I always sat next to Dad as he helped me and cheated for me.

What props we used

Most of our games were dice games which consist of two dice, little men and cards which you had to pick up if you land on a special place.

What I learnt

One thing that I learnt was that however old I was I mustn't cheat because I was the youngest. I always thought that the rules should be twisted about but half the time, especially if I was playing with my brother, I had to keep to the rules.

Also I learnt my numbers and I learnt to count easier.

Play categories

PLAY PROJECT

Imaginative play based on real life	Imaginative play based on fantasy	Creative
Mothers and Fathers	Kings and Queens	Dough
School	Cowboys and Indians	Water
Doctors and Nurses'	Cops and Robbers	Sand
Shopping	War	Mud
Getting married	Witches and Fairies	Clay
	Ghosts	Junk
	Space	Paint
	Monster and Magic	

Constructive	Physical play	Intellectual
Lego	Climbing	Listening to stories
Puzzles	Riding bicycles	Looking at books
Posting Box	Running	Reading
Making models	Hopping	Drawing
Sewing	Skipping	Colouring
Knitting	Head over Heels	Writing
Bricks	Leap Frog	Board games
	Handstands	Card games
	Ball games	Making music
	Swings	Collections
	Slides	Chemistry sets

Research guide to project on children at play

1 Prepare six different sections in your file and use coloured paper if possible. Head each one with a different play category.

Display on each sheet pictures of children involved in the appropriate play activity.

You will find pictures in magazines.

You may draw some.

Use photographs; perhaps photographs of yourself playing or take some photographs yourself of children at play.

Under each picture:

(a) Suggest age of child or children playing

(b) Describe the activity they are involved in

(c) Say what in your opinion is the learning value of the activity

(d) Suggest possible adult involvement in the activity – this could have occurred before play began or may only involve adult in helping to clear away. Comment if you can on how the adult could extend the activity: by suggestion or maybe by introducing a new material or teaching a new technique.

2 In each play section include an observation of child or children involved in appropriate play. Say where the game includes different play categories in the one game.

3 Using the printed sheet which shows the play categories and lists possible play activities *choose* from the *four* different lists the one play activity that you remember playing as a child.

I suggest that you record this play information under the following headings:

(a) Title – include the age you were
(b) What I did (what happened in your game) and where you did it
(c) Who I involved in my game and what I used
(d) How I felt when playing it
(e) What I learned and what rules I had
(f) Adult involvement.

You can use other headings when writing about your play if you want to.

4 Design an indoor and an outdoor play area suitable for pre-school children. List the large and small toys that would be appropriate.

Suggest ten book titles that would interest this aged child. *Important* – don't forget to make provision for the storage of the toys.

5 Visit a children's playground. Spend at least an hour there, and:

(i) Make a *drawing* of *all* the apparatus and other facilities in the playground.

(ii) *Look at* the following facilities:
(a) Toilet
(b) Refreshment
(c) First aid
(d) Safety
Discuss these with the Park Keeper – supervisor

(iii) What is the *role of the adult* in the playground?
What possible functions can he have?
Is there anywhere for adults to sit? *What part do adults play in what the children are doing?*

(iv) *Observation*
(a) Describe the kind of play that goes on, on each piece of apparatus or in the sand pit.
(b) Observe *one* child for at least half an hour and record what he does – comment on what you see.

(v) What is your *opinion* of the playground?

(vi) *Suggestions* for improvement.

The two year old: development guide

Physical development
A two year old can walk steadily and run with flat feet.
Can climb onto furniture and get down again.
All two year old's love wheel toys which they can pull or push.
A two year old walks backwards.
Squats more than sits.
He is constantly on the move.
He likes to walk, run into corners of tables, beds, etc.
Can throw a ball, but only over head. He will try to kick a large ball but will walk into it instead.
He will ride a tricycle by pushing it along with his feet on the ground.
He will build with bricks. The first thing he will build is a tower. He will then push it over.
He loves to scribble, this leads to reproducing the world around him.
He will feed himself with a spoon.
He will try to dress himself. Some things he can do with patience, others he can't.
He may become very angry and frustrated at times.

Speech
By two a child uses 50 words or more.
He puts words together to make short sentences, eg Will not, I know, Yes please.
He talks to himself while playing, and will also join in with nursery rhymes and songs.

Social behaviour
A child loves to be helpful, eg fetch things, dusting.
He should be potty trained, or learning at the age of two.
He is constantly demanding attention.
He will have no idea about sharing or taking turns. He will experiment with other children by poking, pulling, pushing, biting, or scratching.
He will play happily near children, rather than play with them.
He may have Temper Tantrums when frustrated or be angry if, for example, he can't reach something.

Food

He will eat very little, even though he is very active.

So he should be given small amounts of food and leave out any sweet stuff in between meals or rather anytime.

Teeth

A child should have most of his teeth by two to two and a half years old.

He should have 20 milk teeth, which should be brushed twice a day with a flouride toothpaste.

He should eat raw pieces of apple and carrots.

Safety

A two year old is very inquisitive. He will poke, look, climb, and can reach things far away.

He will swallow things that are supposed not to be swallowed, eg buttons.

Keep well out of reach things that might fall onto him, eg saucepans, irons.

A two year old has **very little idea of danger** so must be closely supervised.

Appearance

He will usually look scruffy and dirty, have sticky fingers and mouth.

He needs a daily bath, and tough, but comfortable, clothes.

Sleep

He needs at least 12 hours of sleep a day.

EXAMPLE

Student's recorded observation of a two-year-old

Jane's development study is particularly well-observed: notice problem with temper tantrum.

Name: ALEX
Birth weight: 3.8kg
Birth place: Hospital

Feeding

Alex's mother breast fed him until he was 15 months old. At about five months he was on cereals, puréed fruits, etc.

Alex needs extra cuddling from mother and a lot of love and comfort at night. He clings to his mother a lot. Sometimes he pushes and shoves his friends. With them he is quite rough. He is very polite with adults and says 'excuse me!' he kisses his little friend who is the same age as he.

Temper tantrums

When Alex has a temper tantrum he holds his breath, goes blue in the face, and passes out. He will push his tantrum to the limit to see how far he can go.

He has these tempers about two or three times a week. Changing his nappy when he is dirty and sore, and he just wants to play, causes tempers. When he is cross he will do anything he wants to do. Once he had a temper tantrum in Waitrose over a tube of Smarties his Mum wouldn't let him have.

His mother used to wonder whether she should leave him on his own when he comes through, or punish him or comfort him. She chose to comfort him. When he comes through he is always confused. He probably forgot what he had done it for.

Speech

He has got a very good speech. He can speak full sentences. He started talking at about ten months. His first word was 'Guy' his brother's name. Then there was 'dadda', 'ball', 'want it'. 'Yes' came a long time after 'No'. If Alex cannot say a word then he would make up his own word for it and expect his mother to understand him.

Play

Alex plays imaginative games based on real life. He would play with little model people. He acts stories that have been read to him. His mother keeps one wall in his bedroom for him to paint or draw anything he likes on it. He draws circles. He knows most of his colours. He draws on cornflake packets or tights packets. He loves newspaper. He rides on his little bike but he cannot reach the pedals yet. He loves climbing things. He jumps on and off sofas and bounces on beds.

Routine

Alex wakes up at about 6.30, creeps into his parents' bed for about five minutes. Then he goes and plays with Guy, his brother, until breakfast time. For his breakfast he has cereal or porridge. He is awake all day and goes to bed at 10.30 with his parents.

Things children fear

At two years old, children begin to develop fears, both rational and irrational. Everyone has fears, disclosed, undisclosed, conscious and unconscious. So it is an entirely natural process. When a child cries, it means that the child is hungry or thirsty, wants the nappy changed or is in some way uncomfortable, or simply requiring love and affection. The competent mother will satisfy these needs but if there is too long a time lapse, the child's natural reactions will be fear and distrust. This is because the child is entirely dependent on the surrounding environment. If this fear and distrust is continually aroused – then the whole future of the child is affected.

There are also inborn fears which are pure instinct and these include fear of isolation, fire, animals, weather, darkness, strangers, sudden appearances, water, rushing figures and fear locked in the soul of other people. These fears can be grouped in ages as follows:

6 to 8 months   Fear of strangers now the child has become used to the parents and other adults and children that surround him.

Up to 2 years   Most children are not afraid of animals until this stage. The fear may be triggered by an actual attack on the child or by the size or movement of the animal in question.

2 years   This is the stage where most children begin to be afraid of darkness, isolation, fire, water, weather, sudden appearances, rushing figures and fear in others. These are instinctive fears rather than fears met in actual experience.

These experienced fears include withdrawal of love and fear of punishment – both of which should be avoided at all costs, as these can make a marked impression on future life. Other fears can be aroused by the parent such as 'The bogey man will get you', or by being locked in a room. Once again these situations should be very definitely avoided as the aroused fears cause the child tremendous harm.

Leaving the door open or light on and closing it or diminishing the light over a long period are the methods that should be used to lessen the fear of the dark. This slow process is the way to cope with fears – talk about them, make gradual steps, forget that clumsy over-forceful treatment or general insensitivity which will only result in serious anxiety and difficulty in making social contacts during future life.

Fears should be examined in some detail by the classes.
Children have at least one fear which might affect their behaviour.
Here are some of them to discuss.

Walking over gutters with holes
Children think that when they walk over drainage or any kind of holes they will fall in. They don't know that big things don't fit in small things. You must try to avoid this fear by saying 'You won't fall in, because you're too big'.

Loud noises which may startle them
Loud noises will scare children, for example, if their first teacher shouts and tells them off it is a very bad start to the school years, and the child will begin to hate school.

Crossing the road with big lorries and cars
Little children think that when they cross a road, the big cars and lorries will not see them, so they need someone they know to cross with them.

Fears of tigers, spiders and snakes
Children are frightened that the big cat might gobble them up and that spiders and snakes will climb on them and bite them.

Thunder and crossing the landing at night
Thunder and lightning goes back to the loud noises. The thunder will go bang very suddenly and make children jump. Some children are scared of crossing the landing because of dark and creepy shadows.

The Three year old: development guide

Social development

The three year old child is delightful with no negativeness and awkwardness such as the two year old has. Three year old children have minds of their own but, with understanding and kind management, they are co-operative and eager to please. They still get into trouble but they can learn from *kind* discipline. The most important rule in disciplining a child is to be consistent. Do not keep changing your mind! Children of this age play *with* other children, join in, and take turns. These social skills *must* be learnt before the child starts school. If the child attends playgroup or nursery school he or she will learn to be part of a group and also the social skills that go with it.

Physical development

The three year old can stand on one foot without falling and can run and jump. He can often climb stairs with one foot on each step although he will still descend the stairs with two feet on each step. The three year old should be able to ride a tricycle. He will have good hand and eye co-ordination and will be able to help you carry out relatively simple things, eg setting the table without breaking anything. If you have given your child a chance to practise, dressing and undressing should now be mastered. But the child will still get things on back to front and will need help with buttons and laces.

Emotional development

The three year old can use imagination. The child may talk to a teddy and apply emotions to teddy, eg 'Teddy can't go to sleep'; he won't admit his own fear. Toys are often a go-between for parents and children. Children also begin to act like adults in their play and use real situations, eg a house.

Children of this age are constantly asking questions and the parent should try to answer them in clear terms. They will also begin to be interested in the difference between the sexes. All their questions should be answered clearly, directly and honestly.

Three year olds will know and be able to repeat nursery rhymes. They also love stories and like hearing about their naughtiness when they were younger. At this age they begin to remember things and will be able to understand terms meaning past and present, eg next year, last week, today.

One major development in the three year old is that change can be coped with.

Play

Children love imaginative play, such as shops, hospital, mummys and daddys. Dressing up clothes are an essential part of the three year old's playthings, eg old dresses, hats, shoes, handbags, etc.

They will be able to do simple dances such as ring-a-ring-a-rosy. They will also be able to make a 20 piece jigsaw puzzle as well as play with Lego and other construction toys.

EXAMPLE

Student's recorded observation of a three-year-old

Routine is particularly important for small children as it gives them a secure framework. Emily made the following observations on three-year-old Paul, who was her child study. Notice the comments she makes which give you insight into the way Paul feels about things.

Routines

PAUL

At night after his tea Paul likes to play with his toys for a while and then to sit down with his Mum and Dad to watch television.

At about 6.30 to 7.00 Paul's Mum makes him a cup of hot chocolate. When he's drunk that Paul goes to bed.

First of all his Mum takes Paul upstairs to have a wash. Paul enjoys this because he can show his Mum how clever he is. He said 'Look Mum I've washed my face, and all the soap's off'. When he has had his wash Paul comes down stairs to say goodnight to his Dad.

His Mum takes him to bed and talks to him for a while about what sort of day he had at school. After that his Dad comes up to read him a story. Paul's favourite story is the Three Little Pigs and while his Dad is reading Paul a story he is very excited and when it comes to a certain phrase in the book Paul always shouts it out to show he knows it.

Paul nearly always falls asleep before the story is finished and his Dad ends up reading to himself!

Paul is a very energetic little boy and loves to play and run about. This is why he always sleeps well.

In the morning his Mum gets up about 7.00 and starts getting breakfast ready, Paul usually wakes up between 7.00 and 7.30. When he is up he runs to his Dad and says 'Hurry up dad – be late'. After they have had a bit of a play around Paul goes to get washed. His father is usually in the bathroom so he makes sure Paul washes himself properly.

After breakfast Paul goes upstairs to get dressed. He can manage quite well on his own but likes his Mum to be there, again to show her that he can do it himself.

While Paul is getting dressed his Mum asks him what he will do at school that day and he chats away telling her what he does.

When Paul's dressed he comes down stairs to play with his toys for a while. I think he enjoys his play in the morning because his mind can think and react quicker, so he imagines things better then than at night. I think Paul is one of those children who have to have a little time to themselves in the mornings in order to wake up properly and unwind.

At the moment Paul doesn't have to get anything ready for school, because he only goes mornings. He has to be there at 9.00. His Mum always takes him even though it is only about five minutes walk away.

At about 8.45 Paul and his Mum set off for school. They always call in for Paul's friend, Laura. She lives a little way down the road.

As they are getting to the gate Paul and Laura run off by themselves, but his Mum always waits at the gate until the whistle goes. When it does Paul runs over and says 'You can go now Mum its all right'.

If his mother didn't wait, I think Paul would be quite upset and may even run back to her. Even though he seems quite happy to run off and play with his friends, he still likes to know Mum is there.

By the time his mother has got back home and done some housework it is nearly time for her to go back and get Paul. This is about 12.30.

When Paul comes out of school, he hardly notices his Mum, He runs past her saying 'Hello'. Then Paul and Laura walk home ahead of her. When they get in Paul has his dinner and usually just plays around with his tortoises, whom he has called Miss Baines, who is his teacher, and Fred Stenning, who is his grandad!

Facing up to the birth of the new baby

Facing up to the birth of a new baby at any stage in a child's life can cause the child hurt and bewilderment – a jealous unease that can linger into adult life. Parents often decide to have their children close together in the belief that this will make them close to each other and that they will have someone to play with. This thinking can be mistaken: to face an 18 month old, or two year old with a new brother and sister at a time when they are at the most *difficult* and *demanding* stage of development, needing much patient guidance from the adults, can delay and sometimes retard the maturation process and establish a combative personality. Whenever I ask a group of students which brother or sister in their family they get on with best – it is always the one who is some years older or younger – never the one who is a year or two older or younger than them. It is the latter with whom they have always argued, fought, and towards whom they still feel a strong sense of resentment. Speaking to parents I often find that what they find most upsetting in bringing their children up is how much their children fight, how watchfully jealous they are of each other, especially if they are close to each other in age. *It is easier for a child to accept the intrusion of a sibling if he can talk and has begun to enjoy contact with people outside the home.*

The three year old fits these categories, which is why I pause at this stage to consider how to cope with the arrival of a new baby in the family. Facing up to a new baby will produce great insecurity in a three year old unless every aspect is fully and carefully explained. If it is not, the insecurity will soon turn to jealousy and the older child will draw attention to himself through difficult behaviour. He may also regress: start to want to wear nappies, drink from a bottle, wake at nights, insist on being carried, become clinging and whiney. This is a perfectly normal reaction. Parents need to show patience and understanding but so should relatives and friends! It is very hurtful for the older child if friends and relatives rush to admire and make a fuss of the new baby, bringing gifts. It is so much kinder to greet the older child first, get him to show the baby off, take an interest in what *he* has been doing and bring a small gift for him as well.

My younger son is adopted. The day I brought him home, I had invited my three-year-old's best friend to play, thinking that his company would compensate my son and divert his attention from the time I would have to spend with the new baby. As I was giving the baby his first feed in our home – in walks my son and his friend covered from head to toe in finger paints. So I found later was the sitting, room, not to mention the hand prints up the stairs.

The following guide should help to indicate the steps that should be taken to familiarise the child with the approach of the new baby:

1   Do not tell the child *directly* you are pregnant as he or she has no sense of time and will expect the baby to arrive immediately!

2   Make sure the child is made aware of the impending baby through stories.

3   Make sure the child has a role to play in the preparation for the new baby, eg renovating cot.

4   Do not let the child feel a sense of loss. For instance if the mother is not feeling well, then ensure someone is available to deputise for an outing.

5   Children at three years old ask sexual questions directly without inhibition. Try to answer their questions directly, without embarrassment and in as an uncomplicated a way as possible. I remember a friend of mine's little boy was in a supermarket with very pregnant mum when an acquaintance asked if the little boy was ready for the stork to arrive'. She was somewhat taken aback when the child gave her a blank look, and exclaimed 'that's not how it happens!' and proceeded to give her a graphic description of the entire conception and birth process!

6   The child *must* see the mother in hospital but, for the first visit, it might be better *not* to see the baby in her arms in case of immediate shock jealousy.

7   Remember to give the child a present when the baby comes.

8   During feeding, read to the child, for the baby will enjoy hearing the sound of the mother's voice. *Accept* the feeling of jealousy and anger – they are perfectly natural.

9   Jealousy will not always be aroused at the onset as the baby is obviously

inferior, it becomes apparent when the baby starts moving about and is beginning to talk.

10 The father should enlarge his own role here and make sure he takes the older child for outings and does more grown-up activities with him.

EXAMPLE

Student's recorded observation of the development of sibling relationship

Louise's comment on the observed relationship between Sasha and Zoe show the pleasures and hint at possible problems later.

With Zoe

Zoe is Sasha's seven-month-old baby sister. It is obvious just by watching them together that they love each other immensely. For example, when their mother was preparing dinner she put Zoe in her cot and put Sasha on her bed with me for a story. Zoe was in her cot at the opposite side of the room.

I began reading a book (*Mr Clumsy*) and half way through, Sasha exclaimed 'Oh look what Zoe's doing'. I looked, Zoe was standing up in her cot, supported by the frame, taking chunks out of her cot's paintwork. 'Well,' I said, 'what shall we do with Zoe?' Sasha replied 'Let's have her over here with us for the rest of the story'. So I took Zoe from her cot, sat back down on Sasha's bed and put Zoe on my lap and started again with the story. But that didn't last for long as all Zoe and Sasha wanted to do was cuddle and tickle each other. This kept them happy for 15 minutes – it would have carried on for much longer had it not been dinner time. Zoe and Sasha sat on opposite sides of the dinner table but even this didn't act as a barrier of love and affection. All through the meal Zoe was laughing or grinning, because Sasha kept saying 'Zoe, Zoe, Zoe' very fast and pulling funny faces.

The only time that I have ever seen any conflict between them was when I bathed them. Sasha and Zoe always have a daily bath together. The argument began when Sasha snatched a pink plastic saucepan from Zoe. Hearing Gill's stern voice Zoe began to cry, which made their mother very angry. Although she was told to, Sasha wouldn't hand the toy back. Her mother eventually had to take the saucepan from Sasha to hand back to Zoe. This made Sasha cry and she went into a sulky mood, not wanting to be washed, or to play with another toy. The only thing that cheered her up was her teddy which is a puppet glove flannel.

At the moment Sasha doesn't resent Zoe in any way because she has no reason to feel jealous of her as she can't walk, talk or do hardly any of the things that Sasha can do. *But when Zoe begins to walk and talk and people begin to take more notice of her this is when Sasha may begin to feel a little left out and resentful and when she begins to interfere with her games.*

Now Sasha feels more superior to Zoe than she will, in say, two years time. This is because in this short period of time the age gap will have seemed to have closed quite a lot. Sasha doesn't see herself as another baby competing with Zoe but as a third parent, eg when Zoe drops something Sasha will say 'Ooooh Zoe' in her, 'you are a nuisance', voice. Letting Sasha join in with baby helps turn any resentful feelings into those of co-operativeness and love.

The Four year old: development guide

Once the four year old has mastered speech, he needs a series of new and challenging experiences with which to use it. These could include flying kites, visits to places of interest, outings to the woods and – essentially – people to talk about these experiences with. The child can also express his attitudes by painting or making models.

It is essential to channel the child's interests at this stage or he will become destructive, hyperactive and very frustrated. He will flaunt or challenge adult authority – usually the mother's because of the proximity.

Now the four year old can pedal a tricycle properly, use a knife to spread jam, will be completely toilet trained and will go to the toilet alone. The child will also brush his teeth unguided, but will need help with difficult fastenings. He can be trusted to play outside in the garden and alone with other children. The child will play co-operating with these children and will expect to take turns. Complicated pretend games will be played and he will inevitably be asking adults questions, always asking why – what – how. The child will need factual books to be read on subjects that interest him. In sentences there will be a tendency to leave some words out.

Physical development
The child can run forwards, backwards, sideways and is *very steady on the feet*. The child likes playground facilities such as swings, the slide and climbing frame, but he should always be supervised.
He can ride a tricycle using the pedals, throw, kick and catch a big ball.
He is also skilful with his hands and can thread large beads onto a string.

Play materials are very important at this age:
They like things to thread like cotton reels, or buttons.
They can do easy jigsaws, but they need to be shown what to do. If you are buying the child a toy it must be one that the child will be able to cope with, because if it is not he will lose interest.

The child loves drawing and painting
Place a large sheet of newspaper or waterproof sheeting on the kitchen floor. Then the child can paint away without spoiling the carpet. Painting is expressive play.

Speech

A child at this age should be able to *speak clearly* enough so that a stranger knows what he is saying. He should be able to say several hundred words and will be able to use most words as he wishes.

A child who can speak clearly will not become frustrated, so undue aggression will not be prevalent. Girls usually speak earlier than boys because they tend to observe more than physically playful little boys.

At four the child is always asking questions and these questions need to be answered clearly and simply. Now is also the time for the parent to give reasons for the child not being able to do something.

Four year olds love singing songs and listening to stories and this helps with language development and imagination.

Children will love to dress up in clothes, and they can use large cardboard boxes as ships, or cars, or buses.

They become confused about what really happens and what they fantastise. If the child comes to a parent and reveals something that never really happened – play along with it – it is wrong to call a child a liar because the child is trying to create an impact on the adult by grabbing their attention.

To gauge fully the emotional development of a child it is very important to see things from a child's point of view. If this is not done, their behaviour can be seriously misinterpreted. The relationship between adult and child must be a perceptive compromise, for the adult is guiding the child between right and wrong.

If the child is punished, say by a beating, then he will understand that it is perfectly acceptable to be a bully. The Incredible Hulk is rather like an angry adult to a child and this image is one that is all too common. Children do not have the experience to know the consequences of their actions and unless they are sensibly guided, they will suffer considerable anxiety. Parents who expect the child to have adult reactions, ie 'You know this makes me unhappy' or 'You only do it to make me miserable', are not understanding the child's point of view at all.

Students recollect incidents from childhood

In the accounts which follow, students recall specific incidents from their own childhood. Whilst remembering clearly their own feelings as a young child, they are now able to comment on the situation from a more mature point of view. This 'two-way' viewpoint of a situation can help them to gain a deeper understanding of problems arising with young children, and consequently lead to a wiser response when difficulties occur.

One of these accounts does in fact give a student's observation rather than personal experience, and shows clearly how she feels the trouble could have been avoided.

EXAMPLES

EMOTIONAL DEVELOPMENT (ANNA)

Mischief
The most mischievious thing that I ever did was to take a tin of golden syrup from the kitchen cupboard and hide it behind the coat stand. Every day for a while I would go to it and take a spoonful but then I forgot about it and it was left there for about a month. When my Mum found it, it was all mouldy and had got onto all the coats. I did it because I loved the taste of syrup and I wasn't allowed it very often. When my Mum found out about it I had almost forgotten about it, so I was very surprised and then I was very upset and sorry. I remember my Mum really shouting at me and saying I was 'a very naughty, naughty silly little girl'. I think that at the time I did feel I had been treated in a fair way because I was very ashamed.

Anger
The thing that I always got angry about was not getting my own way. If I didn't then I would scream. One day when we went out, my Mum forgot my bottle and I screamed solidly all day.

Tears
The things that most made me cry was other spiteful children. I always cried if a child took something away from me. I cried when I fell over, and if I didn't get my own way.

Being happy
I always remember being happy when I had my bottle, when I was going to the swings or going to my grandparents' house. The thing that made me especially happy was when my cat had kittens and my sister and I played with them in the garden. I was happy in the mornings at the weekends when I would go in bed with my Mum and Dad, and my sister and I would make a nest at the bottom of the bed.

Being mothered
Whenever I hurt myself I remember sitting on my Mum's knee and I remember the smell of witchhazel. If I fell over I always had a 'kiss it better' and a cuddle. If I had a bad dream then I would always remember going back to sleep with my Mum sitting on my bed and then wondering where she was in the morning.

After a bath I remember jumping out into a big soft towel and then being rolled around in it. I remember very well when I was ill. My Mum used to come and sit with me and put cold flannels on my head. I remember being allowed to pick exactly what I wanted to eat and hearing my Dad coming down the steps and waiting for him to come in and say 'Hello' and 'was I nearly better'.

EMOTIONAL DEVELOPMENT (SUSAN)

Mischief

I remember my Mum and Dad went to visit my aunt for the weekend and I wanted to go, but my Mum said that when she came back I could go to work with her, which I loved doing because I got a lot of attention and fussing. My Nan would be looking after me and my sister. I and my sister shared a bedroom and at night when we were meant to be asleep we had colouring contests. All I used to draw was a few lines and then colour in the spaces. Anyway when I ever showed my drawings to my Mum she always stopped what she was doing to have a look. She said they were very lovely and I used to draw her one. So my Mum and Dad went on their trip, I thought I might decorate their bedroom.

I was about five and just starting school. At the weekend my sister went out and I went up to my bedroom equipped. Anyway it didn't turn out very well. My arm got very tired and I started to get messy. I only did a little bit because my sister came up the stairs.

She told my Nan and when my Mum came home my Nan told my Mum. My Mum started shouting things at me. Then my Nan said 'I can remember when you did the same in my kitchen,' then my Mum started laughing. It is a family joke now.

EMOTIONAL DEVELOPMENT WORK GUIDE

Mischief
Recall the naughtiest thing you ever did.
Can you remember what made you do it?
What did you feel when you were discovered?
How were you punished?
Did you feel you were treated in a fair way?
Catalogue all your naughty deeds and comment on the punishment you received.
Write about a time you were punished for something that you had done, but that you did not consider naughty.

Anger
What made you angry when you were little?
How did you get rid of your agro?

Tears
What made you cry when you were small?
How did you feel afterwards?

Being happy
Remember a treat – a good game – a new toy.

A time when you were happy.
Write about your happy happenings.

Being mothered
When you hurt yourself
When you had a bad dream
After a bath on mother's knee
When you were ill
Write about all your mothering memories

Family rituals
Christmas
Easter
Birthdays
Firework night
Halloween
Births
Deaths
In your family how did you mark these occasions?

Understanding behaviour

The way a parent reacts to the demands and needs of a child is influenced by how the adult was responded to in childhood. For instance – if you were smacked a lot as a child you will probably find yourself doing the same to your own children, unless something important happens to change the pattern. A friend of mine told me how her attitude was changed. 'I didn't realise I was being too harsh with my sons, I was treating them as I had been treated. I used to demand obedience from them, no matter what – smack them frequently and shut them up in their own rooms. It was only when I re-married after being widowed that I was made to stop and think. My husband threatened to leave me if I went on treating the children so harshly.'

An unhappy childhood is likely to be repeated in the next generation. A child from a happy home is given a head start in an ability to create a happy home. A child from an unhappy home is bound to have greater difficulties in relationships with other people when grown up. The same sad things that have happened to him will be experienced by his children. It is only by understanding this fact that steps can be taken to improve the situation. We can rid ourselves of the harmful experience of our childhood by understanding ourselves better and by observing and learning about children.

Each child from birth is a separate personality. It is no good saying 'I don't like children with blue eyes – can't we change their colour?' Better by far to accept the child and encourage the positive traits. For instance, I know of one assertive two and a half year old who demanded to board a bus without assistance. Her mother was so flustered by the child's independence that a smack was handed out. But this quality of independence and assertiveness made starting school for this particular child a joyful adventure and she was genuinely puzzled by the other children who were crying and clinging to their mothers.

Problems
The behaviour we expect of children should be reasonably appropriate to their age and their personality. A lot of irritations like:

Spilt drinks
Muddy carpets
Broken ornaments
Lost shoes
Snatched toys

Playing with food

Sucking a thumb

Splashing bathwater, and many other annoying traits happen because of a child's immaturity and a great amount of curiosity.

If these are not directed by the adults into acceptable channels children will find outlets in destructive and aggressive behaviour.

The behaviour may be seen by adults as naughty or socially unacceptable but will in many instances be part of the essential process of learning.

It is important to discover a child's motives. At times children want to:

Defy you

Disobey you

Shock you

Hurt you

Worry you

Infuriate you and goad you to lose your temper.

Probably the most obvious reason for naughtiness is the *resentment* children feel when they are thwarted or disappointed. Children's expectations are exaggerated and their feelings are very strong. Young children are so involved in coping with their own feelings that they cannot be expected to take into account how other people feel. But if the child is treated with consideration, and patience, acceptance of other people will follow: children learn by example.

Children often lack the experience to understand the consequences of their actions, eg when they say no to an adult, if there is a safety hazard connected with their action, the value and ownership of objects they wish to handle. Neither do they know that it is wrong to steal. It is the adult's responsibility to make an appropriate response when the child experiments and tries out different patterns of behaviour.

Learning by experience

Just as the child experiments with sand and water – many times trying out a sequence to test if the response was always the same – so does the child experiment with behaviour sequences. It is important to appreciate the child's need to experiment during the process of learning – and to understand the difference between acceptable and unacceptable behaviour. To assist the process the adult needs as often as possible to:

Remain consistent in response

Spot trouble in advance

Prevent clashes

Provide distractions and find acceptable solutions

Even when a child of this age does appear 'deliberately naughty' part of the reason will be the child's inability to see the world from the adult point of view and experience.

Faced with the consequences of his action the child is very upset and full of regret. This genuine feeling felt by the child is a better foundation for educating him to avoid similar situations than relying on punishment which can often turn those genuine feelings of regret into resentment.

One six year old was left in an empty newly decorated and carpeted room with strict instructions not to touch a pot of paint left there. The desire to dance in the empty sunlit space was too much for her and, needing something to spin, she picked up the only available object in the room – the paint pot with a handle and began to circle the room. As she gathered momentum the lid of the pot flew off and paint spilled on the carpet. She was immediately overwhelmed with remorse. At this age spontaneous feelings will overcome the force of an adult's instructions – so it is part of the adult's responsibility to try and avoid putting the child in a situation where such conflict may arise. For instance, it would be unrealistic to leave a child of this age alone in the street saying 'only cross to see your friend when it is safe'.

Most children can become obedient and learn socially acceptable behaviour if they have a mixture of:

Love
Stable routine
Being kept busy
Good health and a small amount of punishment.

Punishment
The adult must bear in mind that if a punishment for a misdeed is too severe, it takes away from the child's understanding of what he has done wrong.

The excessive punishment also stops the child from thinking about the cause and focus too much on the punishment itself.

There should not be any punishment for real mistakes and accidents and lots of praise helps a child succeed. Blame and grumbling only makes them nervous and clumsy. The most valuable learning asset is the child's desire to please.

The main points to consider when punishing children are:

Does the child know he has done wrong?
Does he know what he is being punished for?

Has the child really done wrong or just annoyed the adult?
Why did the child do the wrong things?
How does he feel about it?
Has he punished himself by feeling remorse?

All development happens in stages. Each stage has to be gone through successfully before the next can be reached. Children can become *trapped* in a stage which can ensnare them even into adulthood. After 18 months, a child's individual character is beginning to emerge, and how the adult responds will affect the child's perception of himself and his world. Head-on collisions and threats will only confuse and prolong the negative self-assertive without a common-sense stage. Offering alternatives will speed its passing.

Some adults have not learned to cope with frustration, they frequently become angry and excuse their behaviour by saying 'I have a quick temper'. What has really happened is that the adult never successfully *emerged* from the temper tantrum stage of childhood.

We can all revert back to an earlier stage of growing up – and adults often do this when they are ill or under stress. Sometimes the babyish behaviour of a three or four year old is a cry for the remembered comforts of being a baby.

Regression may happen in other ways. A child can revert to bed wetting, remembered food fads, returned reluctance to be alone, thumb-sucking – as well as other kinds of behaviour. All this says 'let me act as a baby for a bit'. The onset of regression may be caused by a new baby in the family, a visit to a hospital, separation from parents, new demands at school. Whatever it is – adults should be prepared to accept and go along with regression. The child will need to feel reassured before he is ready to resume more mature behaviour.

A look at some stages of development in behaviour
A baby needs food when he is hungry and comfort when he cries.

A baby's impression of the world is spoilt if he is repeatedly left to cry because he is cold or hungry, and is seldom cuddled or talked to.

A baby cannot begin to control his behaviour until he recognises his mother as a separate person who is pleased by some things he does and not by others! This stage does not arrive until about the end of the first year.

Children learn to be independent by being allowed to be dependent for as long as they need. All children need a trusted person they can turn to for without them they feel insecure.

After 18 months a child's individual character is beginning to emerge. The child discovers that the adult can be defied, and how the adults respond will affect the child's perception of himself and his world. If this reaction upsets the adult, ie the refusal of food, then the child will feel a sense of power – and an interesting game begins. Head-on collisions can occur over:

Choosing clothes
Eating food
Sharing toys with visitors
Time for bed

Refusing to stop playing in a playground to go home
Refusing to get out of the bath
Demanding sweets in a supermarket

This negative 'No' stage of development reaches a peak about the age of two and gradually by two and a half to three tails off. The child's individual character is now beginning to emerge and the adult response to the challenge of the two year old will affect the child's growing ideas. Threatening and confusing the child will only prolong this stage. Offering acceptable alternatives will help it pass. If the child is handled with understanding, consideration and given definite limits, by three, co-operation and consideration can be mutually achieved.

Temper tantrums

Children do not start off having tantrums in order to get their own way, but they may quickly learn that a tantrum is a good method of getting something they want. Children who hold their breath in a tantrum can use this factor to get their parents to give in to their demands.

A child's tantrum is a cry for help: 'I can't cope' – 'I can't deal with this awful feeling inside me'.

So the child will: yell, scream, kick, hit, bang his head on the floor, throw toys about, tear up newspapers, scribble on walls, shout 'I hate you', 'go away', 'I want', etc.

Being out of control, letting feelings burst forth unrestrained is a frightening experience. Most mature adults keep their feelings well under control, and only let go in their dreams. They usually wake up shaken. Those adults who proclaim that they have a terrible temper which they cannot control are trapped in this early stage of development.

Children's feelings are very intense, their desires very acute – the more strongly a child wants to do something, the more likely serious conflict will occur.

Children are most prone to tantrums from 18 months to two and a half years because they have not acquired common sense and there are many things that they want which they can't have, can't do or can't understand.

A tantrum may be the result of frustration built up over minutes, hours or even days. It is also much more likely to occur if the child is bored, tired, ignored, jealous, anxious or hungry.

These events do not necessarily cause a tantrum but they make a tantrum more likely when conflict arises.

When a tantrum is 'brewing' the child's attention needs to be *diverted* to something interesting to do. If this tactic does not work and a child has a tantrum, accept the cry for help and stay calm, try to talk to the child about his problem and feelings. He will scream, kick, express hatred, but he will regain control more quickly and accept comfort and reassurance if the adult refuses to give up – a very difficult thing to do; as is not giving in to a desire to have a bigger, better tantrum oneself to show the child who is boss – but if this happens it reinforces such behaviour showing it is acceptable – adults do it too!

Many adults feel that a smack puts a stop to a tantrum. But this only adds to the build up of bad feelings which are the underlying cause. On the other hand, to ignore the child is to make him feel rejected and indicate your unwillingness to help. A child sent to be by himself when a tantrum occurs will become *more* distressed and may damage himself and his surroundings. The child's room should *not* be used as a punishment room. Instead it should represent security and reassurance.

Recently I watched an 18 month old child have a temper tantrum at an airport. The family had had a long wait, the child's routine had been disrupted, he was tired and bored. The mother took him into the toilets to comfort him and take him away from the disapproving glances of the people around. When she returned with the child the tantrum was over but his face showed how much the experience had disturbed him.

Watch the child's routine
Make sure he goes to bed early and so is not overtired. Intersperse the day with quiet time, eg listening to a story, colouring.

Children become very irritable when they are hungry, so make sure they don't go without food for long periods.

Make sure you give the child attention during the day by chore-sharing and letting him be generally useful.

Security
Children need to know what you expect from them – without such knowledge they feel insecure. They need to know that an adult is in charge. It is the adult who must decide:

When it is bed time
What is watched on television
What activities are permitted in the living room

Some of these 'limits' are arrived at because they are in the child's best interest, because of safety or well-being. Some also apply because they are necessary for the convenience of the other members of the family. Because children are noisy, boisterous and full of curiosity you have to work out a compromise between the adults' need for:

Occasional peace and quiet
Safety of possessions
The child's desire to experiment and express himself.

If a child associates bed time only with fear of separation and loneliness or anxieties about monsters and witches he will obviously show great reluctance to go to bed and will attempt to postpone the event.

Often a conflict will arise at a time when a relaxed and peacful atmosphere should be more in order. In families where such conflict is generally avoided, the adults have always been prepared to spend time at bedtime with the child and have a bed-time ritual which is repeated each evening.

Such a ritual could include a set time for going to bed to which the child is accustomed, and a series of activities to which the child looks forward, ie a bath with time for play and chat.

Many people's early mothering memories recall the pleasures of being lifted from the bath, wrapped in a bath towel, cuddled, dried and powdered. This would usually be followed by the reading or the telling of a story. The concluding night-time ritual usually involves leave taking and the presence of their comfort toy, blanket or dummy.

Consistent standards

A child becomes confused if his parents each demand totally conflicting standards of behaviour. It is unhealthy for the child and for the parents as the child will be able to enlist one adult as an ally against the other. Children do not like to feel different, they want to fit in and be liked. Consequently, they feel happier if their discipline matches that of their friends at school. A child's happiness depends partly on his ability to associate with other children and adults.

Learning by example

Most of the child's learning about behaviour towards other people comes from the way people are seen to behave: as adults we have to set a good example.
Ask children nicely to do things.
Don't keep shouting at them.
Say 'Please' and 'Thank you' to them.
Be careful of their toys, however old and unimportant they may seem to you; the child may place the same value on them as you do on your most prized possession.

It is a mistake to interrupt without warning a child's activity, which is absorbing and compelling. Children also need help with learning about tidiness and it is wrong to insist that a two year old clears up his toys. Do it with the child and the habit will be developed by the time he is seven.

It is not a good idea to gossip or abuse your friends, the child's teachers or your relatives, in front of the children: They will become confused and stop showing respect for adults.

In one household, a mother answered the phone and told her husband it was his mother on the phone to which he replied: 'What does the old cow want?' When the three year old was called to the phone to speak to his grandmother he said 'Hello old cow'. He was promptly smacked, shouted at and sent to bed. This was a very bewildering experience for the child.

When the child observes what is going on, ie his parents showing concern for their neighbours, a loving and caring attitude to each other, this will be accepted as a pattern to imitate.

It is very tempting to laugh at children, to tease them and make fun of them. Whenever we are tempted to do so, we should pause to think what affect our teasing may have on the child. Is it going to make the child grow in confidence? Develop his understanding of how an adult ought to behave?

Teasing can be cruel and wound the child's delicate confidence rather like pushing a nervous child into the deep end of a pool. One seven year old girl, was sitting down to a family get-together tea. An uncle had wrapped a piece of wood in the same wrapping as the chocolate biscuits and gave it to the child. Shyly she unwrapped it, conscious of many eyes on her and bit into it. There was a great explosion of laughter from the people at the table – making the girl awkward and bewildered, wishing herself invisible. I met that little girl when she was a woman in her middle years. She was a most competent and capable person, but who suffered dreadful embarrassment if she had to eat with people. Teasing has left an emotional scar which she had to carry for life.

As long as a child feels loved he can take his parents' imperfections in his stride and learn self-discipline. If the child's home is basically miserable, where his parents do not care for each other and cause confusion by separate demands, then he will find it much harder to:

Trust others
Sympathise with other people's motives and needs
Appreciate other people's rights which understanding is the basis for genuine good manners.

Some children behave like 'spoilt' children because they have indeed been 'spoilt' by lack of understanding for their need to play and behave like children of their age. What is important to remember is that adults and children see the world from different points of view. The adult has been a child but needs to get in touch with childhood again.

Understanding behaviour   What have I learned?

1   How does our own childhood affect us when we become parents?
2   'Accept the child and encourage the positive traits'. Explain in your own words what this means.
3   Young children 'cannot be expected to take into account other people's feelings'. What reason is given?
4   Name the causes mentioned for bad behaviour by young children.
5   How should adults respond to bad behaviour?
6   Explain the reasons given why it is unwise to rely on punishment too heavily to deal with naughtiness.
7   What are the bad effects of too severe punishments?
8   The main points to consider when punishing children are given. In small groups think of situations where you have seen a child punished by adults, where there points taken into consideration? After your discussion write about two examples saying whether you thought the punishment was appropriate and whether the points had been considered.
9   Give some examples of regression.
10   How should the parent respond to regression?
11   Between about 18 months and about three years, the child challenges the adult. What response is suggested?
12   What action should the adult take to deal with a tantrum?
13   What should the adult NOT do in dealing with a tantrum?

14 The importance of the child's daily *routine* is stressed. Imagine a parent telling a friend about a day with a child and describing the routines. Write down what such a parent should say.

15 Explain the importance of 'limits' on a child's behaviour. Why must the adult set such limits?

16 Why is bed-time ritual particularly important?

17 If a child's parents make very different demands on a child how will it react?

18 Why is it a good idea to be careful with old toys?

19 What is the best way to help a two year old learn to tidy away toys?

20 What is the effect on the child of hearing adults be rude about other adults?

21 What is the likely effect of teasing a child?

EXAMPLES

EMOTIONAL DEVELOPMENT (DEBBIE)
Disobedient behaviour

I am the second oldest with my twin brother. When I was four my personality was a bit like I am now. Because I had a twin brother and also a older brother, I wasn't shy and I use to stick up for myself.

The actual incident

I was about six years old and my Mum wanted to go up her friend's house. I was playing indoors, and she had to take me with her, but I was quite happy at home and I didn't want to go. So then my Mum called me, because I was upstairs and told me to come down, but I just pretended I couldn't hear her. After a little while of shouting to me, she came upstairs and said I was just being silly and if I didn't stop being stupid she wouldn't let me play outside with my friends. I then started shouting at my Mum and I said to her that everytime I went up there she and her friend went off in the kitchen to have a chat and left me in the frontroom bored. Then she went silent for a little while and she said she would phone her friend up and ask her to come round our house, but she wasn't angry with me because she knew I was right.

What motivated me to misbehave in that way

I behaved that way because I was enjoying myself and I didn't want to go around my Mum's friend's house and be bored.

How I felt before and after the incident

Before the incident I was upset and angry because I was enjoying myself and I didn't want to have to go up my Mum's friend's house to be bored.

After the incident I felt silly for arguing with my Mum, because now her friend would have to come over to our house and when my Mum would tell her what had happened she would probably think I didn't like her.

How my Mum responded and the effect it had on me
My Mum was angry at first when I said I didn't want to go but after I told her why she must have known I was right and she then went calm. The response it had on me was I was glad because if I had kept my feelings inside and I kept on going over there, then I would begin to take it out on my Mum and be a very unhappy child, and unable to cope.

My own comments on the way my Mum dealt with the situation
I think my Mum dealt with the situation pretty well because she could have taken no notice of what I had said to her and just made me go, but she listened to what I had to say, and she wasn't angry. Also she sorted the situation in a way that I could still go on playing upstairs while her friend still came round and had a chat.

EMOTIONAL DEVELOPMENT (ANNE)

Disobedient behaviour
A couple of months ago I took my niece down the park, and in the playground section was a little boy of about four or five years old playing quite happily on the slide.

The actual incident
He was as good as gold, taking turns with all the other children, and one little girl couldn't quite manage to get her dress unhooked from the side of the slide. He helped and even let her go before him! But then came his mother marching over and told him that they were going, so that was his last go! The little boy asked if he could stay just five minutes longer, but she pulled him away. Then as she was getting her bag, he ran back up the slide pushing the same little girl away he had helped only five minutes before! He stayed up the top of the slide, and when his mother came back over, and told him to get down, he called her a 'fat old cow' and told her to 'sod off'. His mother didn't find this very amusing and went up the steps after him, forcing him to come down the other end. When she got hold of him again, he kicked her, so she smacked him around the legs twice.

What motivated the child?
I think the little boy acted in this way because he was *rushed* into doing something when he was enjoying himself so much.

How did the child feel before and after?
Before the incident the little boy was so happy and contented. You could tell just by looking at his face.

After the incident he felt cheated and deprived, after all what's five more minutes to a happy little boy?

My own comments
I think his mother acted as a typically domineering and over-powering mother. She could see her son was enjoying himself so why couldn't she have thought first and given him a warning about five minutes before. He would have accepted that, and it would have made things a whole lot easier.

EMOTIONAL DEVELOPMENT (SALLIE)

Naughty, disobedient behaviour

I am writing about one Christmas when I was ten years old. I was living with my step Mum and three step sisters at this time.

The actual incident
My real Mum had asked me what I had wanted for Christmas and I had said a watch. For Christmas she had given me a stocking filled with lovely presents but no watch. The next time I saw her, which was a couple of days later, I sulked. I wouldn't talk to her, I ignored everyone. My Mum tried lots of different methods but none of these worked so in the end she bought me a watch.

What motivated me to misbehave?
I think the reason I misbehaved like this was because I was so looking forward to having a watch and when I didn't get one I was so angry I didn't want my other presents. I don't think my real Mum should have asked me what I wanted for Christmas because I then presumed I was getting a watch.

How I felt before and after the incident
I remember feeling really angry when I didn't get a watch, I just had to have one no other presents would do. When my Mum did finally buy me a watch I didn't want it because every one was calling me spoilt and selfish, and no one would talk to me.

Adult response and the effect on me
When I first saw her and I was sulking she cuddled me saying all my other presents were just as special and as nice as a watch.

EMOTIONAL DEVELOPMENT (VICKI)

Destructive behaviour
This incident involves my sister, she was only four at the time so that made

me nine. She was the youngest and always wanted the attention. She was very irritating and would hide things. She is also very pretty and that won everyone new to the house their attention and flattery. I did not like this and I would tease her.

The incident
We were sitting down stairs on a Saturday morning. There was just me and my sister there, I was having a drink and I would not get my sister one and I would not let her have some of mine. It had been my birthday a week before. I got the usual things, teddys and dolls, all quite nice, but the thing I liked most of all was the wooden recorder that my Dad had sent me. It was the first birthday present I had from him since he left us. I finished my drink and put the cup on the coffee table. Because my sister loves musical instruments and she had none I got my wooden recorder and played every song I could play and also just blew out notes to annoy her. Then all of a sudden she grabbed it out of my hand and screamed, 'I hate you', and smashed it on the side of the table. It broke in two. I grabbed hold of her and possibly could have strangled her if Mum had not come in.

The motivation
The reason she acted like that was because I teased her and annoyed her. She was jealous and she was upset because she never got any presents from my dad. He didn't even know she existed. If my sister had a musical instrument she wouldn't have bothered but I also rubbed in the fact that she never got any presents like me from my dad. It all really boils down to jealousy.

Before and after the incident
I'm sure my sister was hurt and upset before she broke the recorder. She wanted one but she had never got one and I rubbed in the fact and it hurt. When she broke my recorder she felt guilty but satisfied she had made me as upset as she was. If I had not teased her, and let her play with it she wouldn't have done it, but because the present was from my Dad, and it was dear to me, I didn't want anyone else to touch it. It was the first present from my Dad in four years and even if it was a stone I would have loved it.

Adult response and the affects of this
My Mum pulled me off my sister and hit me so hard I was nearly knocked unconscious. She cuddled my sister and said I was crazy. I was crying but I turned and shouted at her to look at what she's done. When I calmed down enough to tell her what happened she told my sister off and told her she must never touch my things. She then told me not to hit my sister as she was smaller than I. My Mum then picked up the recorder and chucked

it in the bin. Later in the evening I got the bits out, I hid them in my room, but they got thrown away when I was about twelve.

The way in which the situation was dealt with
My Mum was right to hit me I think, but she never hit my sister. I caused the trouble and I came out worst off. My sister never got out of my room and always took my things. My Mum was right not to hit my sister at first because she did not know what was going on. I think my sister should have been told it meant a lot to me but then I shouldn't have teased her.

EMOTIONAL DEVELOPMENT (DEBBIE)

Aggressive behaviour
I was roughly eight or nine years old at the time. Because I was rather small and quiet, people would always pick on me and say to me such things as 'Unless you give us your crisps you can't play our game', so I would end up giving my crisps away in order to join in a game. So when this new boy who lived in my street was smaller and younger than me I decided to start picking on him.

The actual incident
This took place in my street and I was wearing my roller skates at the time. I just rolled up to him and started kicking him and pushing him. He ended up having a very bruised leg.

Why I misbehaved this way
I think that I misbehaved this way because everyone used to pick on me because I was quiet so I thought I would pick on someone who has never done anything to me for revengence.

How I felt before and after the incident
Before the incident I had so much anger inside of me that I just wanted to get rid of it, but I had to do it on someone weaker and smaller than I was. After the incident I felt relieved of all my anger but I also knew he wasn't going to let me get away with it, so he went and told his Mum, and then of course my Mum found out.

How my Mum responded and what effect it had on me
My Mum's response to the situation was a very angry one because she had always taught me not to hit other children or start picking on them. My Mum was very annoyed and kept me from playing in the street for two weeks and I was not allowed to play on my roller skates for one month.
  I was very annoyed and angry about the punishment that my Mum gave me because I nearly always got picked on and no one got into trouble for that. At the time I thought the punishment that my Mum had given me

was very harsh because I used to play in the street every night, but now I can see why she did it and it taught me not to pick on other children for no reason and also if anyone picked on me to tell someone then they won't do it again.

My own comment on how the adult dealt with the situation
I think my Mum dealt with the situation quite well because she did not have to hit me, and I think having to stay indoors for those two weeks made me realise to tell someone if somebody started picking on me, and also not to pick on people for no reason at all. So if I had been in the same situation I would have talked to the child and try and find out why she or he did this because he must have done it for some reason, and I would also find out whether he had trouble at school with other children. I still would have punished him though because he could have easily done it again with other children if he was angry or annoyed. I think that I would have punished him the same way, keeping him indoors for two weeks.

NAUGHTY BEHAVIOUR WORK GUIDE

Disobedient behaviour
(a) Refusing to do as told: answering back and even swearing
(b) Not doing as told because of conflicting loyalties or standards
(c) Testing reaction: defining limits

Aggressive behaviour
(a) Frustration: · because child cannot make himself understood – can't reach – can't have
(b) Getting his own back: for unfair treatment – rejection – jealousy
(c) Imitating adult behaviour

Destructive behaviour
(a) On purpose, eg breaking brother's favourite toy
(b) Accidentally
(c) Unknowingly

Remember children sometimes misbehave because they are:
(a) *sending a distress signal*
(b) *attention seeking*
(c) *imitating adult behaviour*
(d) *punishing the adult*
(e) *they are bored*

From each section choose one to do:
1 Give some information about the child, eg age, place in family, personality traits.
2 Describe actual incident.
3 What do you think motivated the child to misbehave in that way?
4 How do you think the child felt before and after the incident?
5 How did adult respond and what effect did response have on the child?
6 Make your own comments on the way the adult dealt with the situation.

The Bogey Man

PART IV

A Guide to Child Study

Child Study – Comprehensive guide

The study of one child should be undertaken *after* a period in which pupils have acquired some knowledge about development, behaviour, and play and have had opportunity to observe children of different ages in a variety of situations. A folder should contain the outline of development of the age of child being studied, and it is a good idea to separate into sections the folder with dividers, each divider entitled with a topic. Each topic can be added to as the study progresses. Photographs of the child and drawings done by the child at different times of the study will enhance the presentation and help to show the child's development. A study to be of real value needs to be conducted over a period of several months. A year is ideal. But a child studied for a shorter concentrated period is also of very great value. Siblings can be the object of the study and often this serves to add a dimension to the relationship. An attempt should be made to see the child regularly, but preferably not always at the same time. So that observations can be made at different times.

Such a study should include observations made by the pupils as well as comments on the observations and also some interpretation of the child's responses and reactions, which will illustrate the pupil's previously acquired knowledge and understanding.

Pupils should remember that they become a very real influence in the child's life and should therefore be aware how they conduct themselves.

1 Never let the child down if an outing is planned or an activity promised unless prior warning is given.

2 Taking a child out on an outing is a great responsibility. Care must be taken and careful preparations made, eg perhaps a change of clothing may be needed, something to eat and drink, money for the phone in case of emergency.

3 Prepare activities that the child will enjoy, eg make some dough, collect scrap materials for making models, make up a book as preparation for an outing, perhaps to the zoo or the local park, invent a game about a favourite television programme, read a story on a cassette, compile a cassette with music – nursery rhymes, make a puppet, etc.

4 Organise a christmas party at your school: invite your child study, cleaners' children, teachers' children, etc. Arrange for an entertainment. Make cakes: prepare jellies, etc. Make paper hats. Make a gift for your child. Import Father Christmas. Prepare your child for this happening, and see him safely home.

5 Always try to see things from the child's point of view.

6 Be prepared to put time and thought into the relationship and the experience will prove very rewarding.

The guides in the book on: Family Data; Emotional development; Mischief; Naughty behaviour; Play; Untruths children tell, which help to put pupils in touch with their own childhood, should be used on the child studied.

A CHILD STODY WORK GUIDE

Observation comment interpretation

Identification
Physical description
Personality characteristics
Home environment
Safety consideration in the home and garden

Family data
See page 39

Routines
Getting up in the morning
Going to bed
Meal times
Shopping
Baby sitting arrangements

Play and social development
Describe under the following headings:

Pretend play based on real life
Pretend play based on fantasy
Creative
Intellectual
Constructive
Physical
Describe what happens in the game
Who did he involve?
What did he use?
How did it make him feel?
What learning value did it have?
Was there any adult involvement?

Where does the child play?
In the house?
Outside?

What toys does he have?
Which are his favourite?
How does he use them?

Where are the toys stored?
How are they stored?
How is the child involved in caring for his toys?
Putting them away?

Observe your child at play
On his own
With one other child
In a group
With adults
With yourself

Special toy
A comforter – can't go to bed without it
A go-between – 'Teddy is afraid of the dark'.
Himself – 'You naughty boy, I am going to smack you.'

Behaviour
Emotional development, see page 129
Mischief see page 130
Temper tantrums see page 136
   What triggered it?
   How did he behave?
   What was adult response?
   What effect did it have on child?
Naughty behaviour, see page 142
   Disobedient
   Aggressive
   Destructive
Untruths, see page 176

New experiences
Starting playgroup
Sleeping away from home
Arrival of a new baby
Going to the dentist
Visit to a hospital

Outings
Playground
Library
Shopping

Zoo
Fun Fair
Seaside
Airport

Museum
Party
Visiting relatives or friends
Holiday

Speech
How well does he speak:
  Distinctly
  Singing words
  Sentences
How does he express his:
  Anger
  Pleasure
  Fear
Does he use polite words:
  Please
  Thank you
  May I?
What childish words does he use for special things – which have become part of the family usage?
Record: Unaccustomed use of words and phrases
  Learn me
  Do-gooder
  A big bath (the sea)
  Misunderstood words
  Stretching word meanings
  Magic words
Make a recorded count of the number of words he knows (if child is under three).

Relationships
Mother
Father
Grandparents
Aunts and uncles
Brothers and sisters
Friends
Yourself
Teacher and other people in authority
Pets

Books
What books does he have?
Read to him
What stories does he enjoy?
Which book does he like to have read most often?

What do you think the appeal is?

When does he get read to?

Take him to a library

Make up a story for him about an outing you are going to have, helping him prepare for a new experience, eg starting school, visiting the dentist, help him to come to terms with something he is afraid of, eg the dark; a bad experience he has had.

What nursery rhymes does he know? Teach him some new ones.

Get him to make a scrap book about something that interests him.

Television viewing

Make a record of a *week's viewing*

Watch with the child his *favourite ones*

Why do you think he likes them?

What does he say about them?

Does he use what he has watched in his play?

What has he learned from the programme?

Get him to *draw* some of the characters and incidents

How much does he remember of what he watches?

With whom does he watch television?

After this summarise what conclusions you have come to about the effect of television on your child study.

Visit child study at playgroup school

Describe the classroom and equipment/Draw a diagram of classroom

Record: Daily routine

What activities child study participated in

His relationships with – teacher/other children

Changes

Having studied your child study for a period of time, take stock:

Looks

New skills acquired

Behaviour

Language development

Difficulties in the child's life

Relationships

Effect of good and bad experiences on understand of the world, people

Keep a diary of all your visits

Record *your observations and impressions* of the experience

What have you found difficult?

When had the child made you angry/aggressive?

How did you control your feelings?

What did you find most interesting and rewarding?

What do you think you have *gained* from the experience?

PART V

Moving into the Wider World

My attitude to school
I thought that school would be really exciting, and I couldn't wait to start, but then when I finally did start I found that I missed my Mum.

Starting school

For any child to negotiate a new experience successfully he needs to be carefully prepared. This is never more true than in getting the five year old ready for the experience of full-time compulsory education. This indeed brings an enormous change in the child's life, especially with a first child and for the parents as well. Hitherto the parents had sole charge and control over their child: when he got up, what he wore, when and what he ate, with whom he played, how he behaved. The law in this country does not interfere unless the child is reported to be in need of care and protection, but when the child reaches the age of five the parents are compelled to send their child to full-time education, which will be compulsory until the age of 16. All too often the first experience is unhappy and it can colour our outlook for a long time to come. Eleven years of school life is a long time to be unhappy. It isn't always these first encounters with school that influence the years ahead but if things go wrong at that stage they are very difficult to put right. Many young people have failed to enjoy school and failed to reach their potential because their first experiences of school had turned them against the system.

Starting school should never be the first separation from mother or the first experience of being a member of a group, so attendance at a playgroup, mother and toddler group, and activities such as birthday parties, outings with other families, staying away from home with relatives and friends, become crucial. The child must not feel that the school is separating him from his mother.

The parent may also feel the forthcoming separation acutely and worry that the attractions of new activities and friends will lure away the child's affections. They will punctuate remarks about school with, 'Will you miss me?,' or 'Will you cry?', thus forcing the child to demonstrate his loyalty through a seeming reluctance to leave the parent and meet the challenge of school.

Many adults have not had happy school experiences, and continue to feel resentment and anger towards school activities and the teachers. On no account should these feelings be conveyed to the child. The child's identification with his parents is so strong he is bound to be influenced and be doomed to share his parents attitudes. Positive aspects of school should be stressed, ie school is a sign of growing up, a place where the child will acquire knowledge and skills, a place where he will make new friends, take part in exciting activities and he will be in the care of competent and caring adults. School will serve to enrich his, and his parents', life. On the other hand, every new experience has good and bad points and if a part of the experience proves to be unpleasant this should be faced honestly but without exaggeration. The reassurance will come from the explanation of how to handle the unpleasantness and the knowledge that the child is supported by sensible and loving adults.

School should never be used as a threat – 'Just you wait till you go to school – they won't put up with this sort of behaviour. They'll sort you out.' Neither should school be described in the child's hearing as providing the parent with freedom from the demands of children or creating exciting new possibilities which the child will miss out on. In fact the child's home circumstances, if at all possible, should remain the same during the time he starts school. It is not a good time for the mother to start a job, because the child's first year at school is punctuated with all sorts of adjustment problems which require very sensitive awareness from the adult as well as the obvious point that frequent infections caused both through tiredness and usual childhood infectious disease, will mean absence from school and will put pressure on a working mother and consequently on the child.

The home routines round the school day must be carefully planned and adhered to, and obviously they cannot be introduced the week before or the child will not accept sudden restrictions – such as going to bed early because he is going to school, if he has always been allowed to stay up. I went to have a meal with friends one evening to find that their three and a half year old stayed up all evening – fractious and in the way – his mother's reasoning for not putting him to bed was, 'Well poor thing, when he starts school he will have to follow a timetable and regulations. I want him to enjoy his freedom while he can'. I was sure he would have enjoyed his mother's undivided attention during a bath and bedtime story rather than the absent-minded and casual attention he did receive – often sought by him through difficult behaviour during the evening I spent at his house.

School life is going to place many demands on the child: for the first time the child will be separated from his parents for the major part of the day. It is therefore essential that time is set aside before and after school for the comfort and support that he is used to. He may well regress at such times demanding help with tasks such as dressing or other requests for individual attention. For this to happen the child and parents need to be awake in good time, which implies an early bed-time, and for the five year old between 6.00 and 7.30 pm. The school routine is often very busy, not allowing very much time for 'individual pace'. But we all need this, and the time at home should provide it; there must be ample time for washing and dressing without risk of conflict. Choice of clothes should have been prepared the night before, together with other necessities such as shoebags, swimming things, dinner money, or reading book. Obviously the child needs time for a good unhurried breakfast. Many children need a play session with familiar objects before they are relaxed enough to start out for the demands of school. Sometimes taking to school a small reminder of home, which can be kept in a pocket, a favourite model car or a small toy animal, can help the child ward off homesickness at school and serve as a reassuring link with home.

It is a very upsetting experience for the child if a parent is not waiting to take the child home at the end of the day. It someone else is going to fetch the child or if the parent is delayed, the school should be contacted and asked to inform the child, otherwise anxiety will be aroused on many future occasions and the child will not be able to concentrate because he will be terrified that his parent will not fetch him.

Children vary on what they need after a school day but many will want to arrive home to a familiar and undemanding situation, uncluttered by visitors; although some children will enjoy company or visiting at this time. It is usual for the child to want something to eat when he finishes school. It is sensible to accustom the child to have 'proper' food, eg brown bread with butter and jam – cereal with fruit, rather than give them sweets or crisps. But whatever activity the child will wish to engage in, he will need a parent available for a lap from which to watch television or to tell about his day or just the reassurance of mother's or father's presence.

Children will adhere to a reasonable bedtime far more willingly if going to bed is something to which to look forward. A leisurely bath with attendant adult will relax the child and often be the time when children will confide problems they may have had, or things they have not understood, or just use it as an opportunity to chat and feel close. A story chosen by them to be read by a parent in the comfort and cosiness of the bedroom, provides much more satisfaction than to be allowed to stay up to watch adult television. The putting to bed at the end of a day will take up at least half an hour, may be an hour, or even longer, but this shared time at the end of the day is a very precious time for both the child and his parents. Children who watch adult television at this stage of their lives have been found to have more anxieties and worries and find it hard to concentrate on their work.

Parents and teachers alike must expect emotional ups and downs at this stage. Children starting school often regress to bed wetting. If the child is on the brink of tears, is being difficult, or having temper tantrums it is a sure sign that he is having a problem. Children often cannot articulate the cause of their anxiety and teachers and parents should be sensitive to these changes and should discuss worries either may have about the child. One shy, quiet five year old felt sick every time she had to eat everything up on her plate at school dinner-time. The anxiety spoilt her whole morning. She started to bed-wet and then make excuses for not going to school – her tummy hurt, she felt sick, . . . The mother, when she discovered the cause of her daughter's anxiety, told her to tell the dinner lady – 'I pay for my dinner, so I'll eat what I want'. When confronted by the dinner lady, frightened though she was, she complied with her mother's directive and blurted out what she had been told to say. The shocked dinner lady slapped her and marched her off to see the headmistress for her cheekiness. These adults in this little girl's life let her down.

If the parents are in disagreement with the school the child cannot cope when faced with conflicting loyalties which he cannot resolve. It is important that such difficulties are resolved through discussion with the school rather than the child.

Important events in the child's life, such as a new baby in the family, experience of hospitalisation, a separation, perhaps a time spent in care, loss of a parent, moving to a new district, death of a pet – all need to be communicated at the school in the child's interest. Young children cannot compartmentalise their lives – what happens at home and what happens at school influence each other. Children cannot learn if they don't feel secure and free of anxiety.

It is very important indeed for children to see their parents take an interest in what they do at school: they love them to come into their classroom to admire paintings or a piece of writing they have done, or share with their parents, for instance the things that are on the nature table. Things that are done at school and brought home should be given pride of place. The child needs his endeavours to be appreciated and valued. However, *it is important not to emphasise the competitive aspect of education* at this stage, eg too many enquiries about which reading book the child is on as compared to other children or is he on the top table for maths, can only cause anxiety, and the child will begin to think that the parents' love depends on his achievement. For the parents also to have their children exposed to the initial appraisal of strangers away from the security and acceptance of the family circle can produce unease, which sometimes can result in rather an aggressive attitude to the school. 'You stand up for yourself – don't let *them* tell you what to do – don't let *them* pick on you' are the instructions parents have been known to give, with unfortunate results for the child, who will find it difficult to accept the teacher's authority, criticisms of his work, and will find it difficult to get on with other children amicably. He will always be on the look-out for slights and demanding his rights.

When the child starts school the child's interests and energies will begin to move away from home life and close relationships within the family to encompass other relationships with children he meets at school and his teachers. Children, in other words, are growing up, becoming more in-dependent. Sometimes parents can view this as a threat and can feel hurt at the child's continuous reference to 'My teacher says'. They should regard the child's ability to make relationships outside the family as their accomplish-ment. Children can only make successful relationships if they are safe and secure in their relationships with the people at home.

Schools are very aware of the importance to children of a good start to the school life, and do all in their power to help. All children are invited with their parents to visit the school before the child starts – they encourage mothers to take them to the lavatory and hang their coats on their special picture peg. The entry is often staggered so you don't get a whole class of children, thus giving the teacher and other children more opportunity to concentrate on the newcomers and make them feel at home. Children starting school go for morning or afternoon school. Only when they are judged ready will they be expected to stay all day at school. Many schools follow the policy of the child's first teacher visiting the child in his own home before he comes to school, thus uniting the two worlds and getting to know the family and their circumstances.

Children who settle well in school and are able to get the most out of it are:
(a)   *Children who mix well with other children*

They have had plenty of opportunity to do so, they have visited their friends in their houses, have had outings to playgrounds and made friends there, and they have attended playgroup. They have had many opportunities to share experiences, such as parties and outings. They have had plenty of good play opportunities provided, eg dressing up, sand, water, ball games, climbing apparatus, building blocks – activities which are fun to play with other children and they have had wise adults to supervise their play; to guide them into *sharing*, *taking turns* and who have resolved squabbles or eased hurt feelings.

(b) *Children who can get on with adults*

Children must be able to trust adults: if the parents have been consistent when they have said 'no', stuck by that and not said 'yes' after the child has nagged them, they will expect adults to keep promises and respect their threats.

Children need to be used to being left with other people and know that they will be collected.

Children need to feel confidence to do as strange adults ask, perhaps climb on apparatus, attempt to learn something new. For this they rely on past experience of trust in adults: mother has left me with this adult so they will treat me well.

They need training in basic good manners, learning not to interrupt conversation, showing respect, showing appreciation for gifts or help offered. The child must be able to accept correction from adults other than his parents without showing resentment.

Parents should avoid answering for their child when adults ask them questions.

They should be encouraged to deal with adults such as the milkman and shopkeeper.

It is not a good idea to gossip about friends in front of children, it will diminish the respect they should be encouraged to have for adults.

There are certain tasks that the child needs to be able to perform independently. He should be used to putting things away after himself and sharing responsibilities for certain family tasks, eg laying the table, feeding pets, helping unpack the shopping.

Be able to dress himself.

Eat in a sociably acceptable way.

Go to the lavatory on his own.

Have had experience of making a choice, eg what to wear, in what order to carry out activities.

Having a good attitude to learning

A child who has been encouraged and praised at home will have confidence to tackle learning tasks at school.

A child who has been talked to, listened to, read to, taken on outings, had rich play opportunities, is used to quiet times in his day to listen to a story or a record, do a painting, play with *Lego*, who can join in conversation round the table, has been encouraged to express his opinion, will have developed the skills necessary to **concentration**, which is the most important skill in any learning.

The following is a suggestion sheet issued by a First School to parents giving guidance about the sort of things they should do with and for their child as a preparation for school:

Ways to help children

Encourage them to do things for themselves – like dressing, going to the toilet, washing and drying their hands.

Help them to recognise colours and shapes that they see around them.

Count with them and use words about numbers – long, short, tall, high, heavy, light, full, empty, wide, narrow, small, smaller, smallest.

Read to them as much as you can. Get them to talk about the story and about the pictures in the books and pick out the details.

Take them out as much as possible and talk about the things you see: the sort of shops – supermarkets, fishmongers, greengrocers; the traffic – motor bikes, makes of cars, tankers, scooters; the plants, trees, flowers, animals; the colours, smells, shapes that are all around.

Talk to them and give them the time to talk back to you. Use lots of words to describe things: don't just say 'There's a cat'. Try and describe it – 'There's a small brown striped cat with a long tail, green eyes, pointed ears and thick fur'. I know that is exaggerated, but you see the sort of thing I mean.

Listen to them and help them say words and sentences properly. Try to get them to say more than one or two words in answer to a question.

Let them help you at home and talk about what you are doing – the soft blankets, the smell of the polish, the noises the sausages make as they are frying, the sharp taste of the lemon, the way the baby looks as he sleeps. There are lots of everyday things the children can help with and, most important, talk about. Talking about what is happening at the moment, what happened yesterday, what is going to happen tomorrow, all help to fix and identify things in the children's minds.

A few reminders

Do come in and visit us before John starts school. This will get him used to the look of things. Be prepared to stay with him for several days when he starts and while he is settling in. Talk about school to him. Emphasise that every day you will be coming back to take him home.

Please be on time to meet him after school. Little children get most upset if they think they have been forgotten, and even five minutes is a long time to them.

EXAMPLE

The recorded observation of a morning at a First School where a pupil went in order to observe her sister on whom she was doing a child study, describes some of the experiences a child is likely to encounter and the children's response to them. Notice particularly the sensitive way in which the pupil responded when a tricky situation occurred in the hall during physical education.

Victoria at school

Victoria goes to Carlton Hill First School. The school is about 10 or 11 years old. Altogether there are only about 100 children in the whole school and that is four classes with about 25 children in each. It includes a nursery class joining onto the school.

Vicky is in an introductory class which means her class has some four year olds and some five year olds. When Vicky reaches six she will go into another class. The four year olds in Vicky's class only go for the morning so they all went home in the afternoon.

Whilst Vicky and her class were watching television in another room, Diane and I were in her classroom taking note of all the things in there which encourage the children to learn, and all the equipment.

There were five desks in Vicky's classroom. Each had their own colour and a picture of the colour of their table. Also the same picture was on their pegs to hang their coats, so they could easily recognise their own one.

There are lots of interesting things on the walls in Vicky's classroom such as alphabet posters, shapes, colours of balloons, numbers, objects, calendar, picture cards with Words to Learn, colourful posters, posters of animals, pictures of nature, flowers, and paintings done by the children even on the windows. The entire room is covered in these things.

There is a nature table with sticky buds and flowers. Each table is growing cress seeds so that the children can watch them grow. All the different kinds of flowers are labelled.

There are shelves with books on, and a rack covered with books, some titles of these books are:

Topsy and Tim go to the Seaside
The Giant Book of Nursery Rhymes
Ben Goes to Hospital
Janet and John Books
Mojo Goes to Town .
A large range of *Mr Men* books
Paddington

There is a lovely Wendy House which takes up one corner of the room. It is hand-made out of wood, inside it is kept immaculate. You can fit about six or seven children in without being cramped together. It is just like a miniature ideal home. Inside there is every little detail. There is: A bed with two teddys in it; A cot with dolls; A pram; A Welsh dresser; A rug; Two cushions; A table with a teaset on; An oven with little pans on rings – a little toy electric one, the rings go red when you turn a knob; A cupboard with pans all shapes and sizes; Two stools; A radio; A telephone; An iron;

A brush, talc, perfume and deodorant; Real curtains at the windows; A clock, oven gloves, tea towels; A drawer full of cutlery.

Near where all the books are there is a big carpet with an armchair where Miss Cull, Vicky's teacher, sits when she reads to them, and when they sing songs, all of the children gather round her on the carpet.

Daily routine

When Diana and I arrived we went straight into the classroom, Vicky dragging us in quickly so everyone could see us. We sat down while Miss Cull called the register. A few of them rolled in late, and they are quite strict with that.

Then they all went to their desks to wait until one person gave out all their tracing books and they each had a little tin with their name on and their own crayons inside. Nearly everyone was showing us how they hadn't broken any of their crayons yet. They traced pictures off cards and then coloured them in. After about half an hour they all put their things away, table by table, neatly in their own table's drawer.

They then all lined up by the door ready for assembly. The girls went in first, Vicky holding onto my hand and another girl onto Diane's.

When they all sit down it is all quiet with good order in the Hall. The children only took up half the Hall. They all say 'Good Morning Mrs Garner' in harmony! She was the teacher of the class who were taking the assembly. It was a class of six year olds who all sat at the front and told a simple story with the pictures they had drawn. They had also made their own books and proudly showed them to the rest of the school.

Then they all bowed their heads and prayed about the world. Victoria looked to see if Diane and I were praying, then she was good.

Then all of the school turned around to sing some songs while Mrs Garner played the piano.

Victoria didn't know the words, neither did many other people in her class, so she just opened her mouth and sang anything! All the time she was watching us and laughing. Then the school filed out, class by class, singing a 'Pitter Patter' song.

PE time

After assembly they came back into the classroom and Miss Cull said 'Right everyone get changed!' They all got changed into knickers and vests and lined up by the door. They then led into the Hall and the different apparatus were already out because some of the older children helped get them out after assembly.

First of all they all gathered round Miss Cull and they all said out loud three simple rules they all knew about their PE lessons. They were:

Use your arms and legs not your tongues
Wait your turn
Don't run; and look where you are going.

Miss Cull blew her whistle and they all went off to do their own things on the climbing frames, bars, ladders and ropes.

Victoria was right in front of us swinging on a bar, she wanted Diane and I to watch her all of the time and was showing off a bit.

A little Chinese boy, Ka Fai, didn't want to do PE. Miss Cull said he never does it and she didn't make him. Diane and I sat with him.

Then they all played 'pirates', a game where they have to climb about the apparatus without touching the floor. There are mats and they were all right. Two people were 'It', and they had to chase people to touch them, then that person was out.

Vicky was all right until half-way through when it caught her eye that Diane and I were making a fuss and playing with the Chinese boy. She came to us and acted all 'soppy' and wouldn't let go of me. She said she didn't want to do PE any more. Then Miss Cull pulled Vicky away and told her not to be silly and the next minute we turned around and Vicky was sulking in the corner, so Miss Cull went up to her and so did Diane and I and I told her we would go home if she didn't do PE then we walked out of the hall and we heard Vicky crying.

So we came back in and I had an idea. I said I'd join in with Vicky in the game and help her, so I did. We ran around, me holding onto her hand. It wore me out! I haven't done that sort of thing for ages! Still, it stopped Vicky.

After PE they came back to the classroom to get changed. And because Vicky came to me to do up the zip on her dress, all of the other children came running to us to help them with laces, buttons, zips, etc!

When they were all dressed they drunk their drinks and ate apples and oranges which they bring to school themselves.

Then they all put their coats on to go out to play on a place like a veranda. It was just Vicky's class as all the classes go out at different times. They had some things to play on and to play with including:

Two spacehoppers
A bike
A wheelbarrow
A climbing frame and slide
A swing
Two rocking horses
A barrell to roll.

Vicky's class had break at 10.40. Victoria played on a spacehopper showing off and she asked Rebbecca if she could go on a swing. Rebbecca let her have a go, so Vicky called to us to watch how high she could go. She wouldn't let anyone talk to us. If they did she pushed them away. All the other children wanted us to watch them do various other things too.

After about 20 minutes they all came in from outside, and Miss Cull said they were going to go to watch television, so they quietly walked through the hall as there was another class doing PE and they went to watch the television in the staffroom. They watch 'Lenny the Lion' every Friday. Diane and I stayed in the classroom to observe the different things.

When they came back from watching the television they all gathered round Miss Cull's armchair in the reading corner on the big mat. The ones who were sitting up the straightest could sit at the back on one of the four plastic reading chairs.

Miss Cull read them a story taken from *The Naughty Little Sister Book* called 'The Wiggley Tooth'. Everyone listened quietly and enjoyed the story. Then they sang some songs until dinner time. They sang: *Hickory Dickory Dock, Sing a Song of Sixpence, Little Robin Redbreast, The North Wind Doth Blow.*

Matthew chose to sing: *Jack and Jill.*

Vicky chose to sing: *Went to the Animal Fair.*

Then they all sang: *I Know a Little Pussy,* and *Horsey Horsey Don't You Stop.*

Then they all lined up for dinner.

Vicky told me off when she came home because I didn't say goodbye to her, but Diane did.

We thanked Miss Cull for having us, and Mrs Rowland the Headmistress. I had to get my Child Study off her because she looked at it and said it was good.

What have I learned?   **Questions on children starting school**

1   Give reasons why a parent may find it difficult when a child starts school.
2   Explain in your own words why it is not sensible for a parent to say 'You will miss me won't you?' when a child starts school.
3   What experiences should be offered a child to ensure that going to school is not his first separation from mother?
4   Why must parents take care about sharing their own school experiences with a child starting school?
5   What positive aspects of school should a parent stress?
6   How does a parent reassure the child when the inevitable upsetting experience has to be dealt with?
7   What warning does the author give remarking to the child concerning changes that school will bring to the child and parent?
8   What home routines should be arranged to help the child cope with school?
9   Why should these be introduced well before the time of starting school?
10   If the parent is unexpectedly prevented from picking up a child from school what steps should be taken to avoid problems for the child?
11   What recommendation does the author make for the time of arrival from school?
12   What are the signs indicating problems at school that a parent should look out for?

13   What is the best way of dealing with such problems?

14   Why is it important for the parent to let the school know of changes in the life of the family?

15   If a child talks a good deal at home about their teacher how should the parents take it?

16   Give examples of ways in which a parent can take an interest in what the child is doing?

17   What bad effects are there if parents place too much stress on the competitive side of school?

18   What must a parent do to ensure the child is able to mix well with other children before starting school?

19   How can children be encouraged to trust adults as a preparation for starting school?

20   List the tasks the child should be able to perform independently before school starts.

21   What can a parent do to encourage good learning attitudes in a child?

22   When children go to school they have the following demands made on them; Suggest how best they can have been prepared to cope with these:

(a)   separation

(b)   coping with the geography of the school building, eg strange space.

(c)   using a wide range of equipment and materials.

(d)   timetable routines: having to stop action when in full swing, clearing away.

Things to do in a group of three or four

1   First of all consider the activities described that Victoria and the other children do at Carlton Hill. Decide what the child learns from each (if anything!)

2   Compare your own experiences of starting school and say whether you agree with the author about how the parent should prepare the child and what mistakes to avoid? Looking back on it could you have been helped to avoid problems? What helped you most in your start?

3   Imagine that each member of the group is to meet some parents of children who will start school in two months time. Each of you has to tell your parents how best to prepare for this important event. You have only **two minutes** to speak to them after which they may ask questions.

Share your ideas.

Individually make notes for your talk.

Give your talks – the other members of the group are the audience and may ask questions after the talk.

You may find it useful to decide who gave the best talk and *why* it was best.

Remember: The parents have to prepare themselves as well as the child, and perhaps the school needs information as well.

Two minutes only.

The five year old: development guide

Physical development
Very active and energetic
Loses rounded 'babyshape'
Walks and runs easily
Skilful in climbing, sliding, swinging
Skips on alternate feet
Dances rythmically to music
Can hop on each foot
Plays ball games quite well and will obey simple rules.

Fine movement
Can thread large needles
Uses a knife and fork
Draws a recognisable figure, with head, body, legs and arms
Draws a house, with windows, doors and chimney.

Speech development
Speech is fluent
Loves reciting rhymes and poems and singing songs
Love to be told stories, and makes up games about them afterwards
Knows own name, address and age.

Has a vocabulary of about 2000 words and uses long sentences. Good speech development is very important by the time the child reaches five for both communication and understanding. Words are needed for the child to think, to wonder and to question. From now on the child must make use of language not only to make sense of the personal world, but also for learning.

Social behaviour
Dresses and undresses (needs help with some things).
Washes hands and face.
Generally more sensible, controlled and independent.
Chooses own friends.
Plays for hours, with friends or alone.
Co-operative with playmates, most of the time.
Understands the need for rules, and fairness.
Shows a sense of humour.

Kind and protective towards smaller children and animals and will comfort friends who cry.

Children at this age are very moral – everything is black or white.

Starting school

Need careful preparation.

Gentle introduction with half a day at first as the five year old quickly becomes tired.

School seems a strange place – busy and organised.

Must get used to teachers and other children.

Most children have developed enough inner self-control to be ready for school, nevertheless they need encouragement from home, to help them settle happily.

This stage of moving into the outside world is very worrying for the child.

Parents and teachers must expect emotional 'ups and downs'. If the child is very 'difficult' or on the brink of tears or tantrum, something is wrong.

Parents can help by making constant contact with the classroom and they must talk to the teacher about any special difficulties, or worries that the child may have. eg new baby in the family, time spent away in hospital or in care, break-up in the family.

Parents should let the child see them in the classroom, talking to the teacher, and looking at the work and paintings on the wall. When the child brings paintings home they should be put up on the wall. The child's interest and energies will move away from close relationships in the family, to close relationships with playmates. Gradually the five year old is becoming more and more independant.

Ailments/illnesses of early school years

During the first year at school the child usually is ill with coughs, colds, sore throats or with the childhood diseases of mumps, chicken-pox, German measles and measles.

Preparing children for going into hospital

All children need to be prepared for the possibility of going into hospital. For some children it is a one-time experience and for others it will become a frequent occurrence. Sometimes children are admitted in an emergency situation.

Fear of the unknown can be removed for the child by familiarising the child with the roles of doctors and nurses, who can be presented in a positive way as sympathetic, caring people, giving the child an idea of what to expect if they are admitted. It is also essential that the child's vocabulary includes words that otherwise carry a frightening mystery: injection, bandage, dressing, anaesthetic, operation, surgeon. Children's play is the best introduction, together with books, stories and parents recounting their own hospital experiences. Props, such as doctor's bag and stethoscope, nurse's uniform, bandages, hospital puzzles, colouring books with hospital themes are all helpful. If the hospitalisation can be anticipated, a preliminary visit to the ward and the nursing team as well as a mock operation on Teddy can be used as preparation.

The truth without exaggeration should always be told otherwise the child stops trusting adults and responds to treatment in a histrionic way in order to convince the adult that it *does* hurt. It is much the best policy to say: 'the injection may hurt for a short time, the pain will soon stop; when its over we'll go to the park to feed the ducks – I will read you a story – you can play with your friend, and you can think about *that* while you are having the injection and how you will tell Daddy/Grandma about it'.

Some hospitals supply activity rooms, with toys and play leaders to help with the problem of boredom. There is no doubt that children who are happy and occupied will make a better recovery. A children's ward in a hospital often resembles a playroom – with many toys such as bikes, prams, dolls houses – opportunities for messy play – pictures children have drawn pinned on walls – with mums and dads, brother and sisters reading to, cuddling, talking with, and soothing a child, and other children whose parents are not there. I can remember wards, with each child in his bed or cot, the toddler strapped in so he couldn't climb out, and a magnificent display of soft toys – untouched – in an entrance lobby. Visiting hours were rigidly kept to – and often I heard the sister turn parents away with remarks like 'don't go and see him, it'll only upset him – we have gone to a lot of trouble to settle him'. At first those children cried and were told that they were 'naughty' – but silent withdrawal and quiet acquiescence is a sign that something is wrong!

Gradually they stopped crying and their cries were replaced with a look of bleak dismay and helpless resignation: they believed their parents had betrayed and abandoned them. The damage caused by such an experience would leave an emotional scar long after any physical scar had healed and sometimes the damage would be permanent. Parents have been known to bring their child to hospital dressed in party clothes – having told the trusting child that they were going to a party – when in fact they were to have an operation or treatment requiring a hospital stay. They didn't do this because they were bad or wicked parents, they did it because they were misguided. I don't think this would happen today, but visiting a child in hospital recently I heard a father say to his four year old son that he had to leave. The little boy protested and clung to his father who, to calm his son down, promised that he would return. The father knew he couldn't return that day – the little boy sat waiting – he wouldn't eat his supper, he wouldn't go to sleep – he kept waiting for his father and as time went on – he cried silent tears. The nurses kept trying to reassure him – maybe the bus was held up – maybe – maybe – but *the father had promised* – and the child waited.

If staying in hospital with the child is not possible, frequent visits should be made throughout the day and evening, but whatever the arrangement the parents make, the child must be told the truth. A screaming protest may be inconvenient for adults to handle, but it is a natural, healthy response.

Little presents brought in often to break the monotony are preferable to lavish gifts. Children regress when they are unwell and prefer the comfort of undemanding activity, perhaps something they had enjoyed doing when they were younger.

Favourite comics, simple puzzles, colouring activities, special pens, a new pencil case, a new pack of cards are all good presents to bring. And, of course, all children need the presence of their comfort toy; sometimes a child will tell you how he is *really feeling* through his teddy – he may not wish to let himself down in the adult's eye as not being grown-up enough to cope. In most hospitals visiting by parents is unrestricted and in some hospitals mothers are able to stay in hospital with the child.

It should not be forgotten that for many children a hospital stay can be a positive experience, giving a sense of achievement. Also the relationship with parents can be deepened allowing a child to relate to a new group of people, therefore adding not only a valuable dimension to life, but also confidence with which to tackle problems later. Nevertheless, when the child returns home adjustment problems may occur, ie, sleep may be difficult in a silent bedroom after the noise of a ward. Regressive behaviour such as bed-wetting or wanting to be 'babyed' will occur.

It is important that the parents mask their anxiety and present a calm, controlled and confident appearance to the child. A little spoiling is inevitable, but if this is overdone the child will associate illness with reward and may make a pretence of sickness to gain attention.

Here is a basic guide to hospitalisation for young children:

Ignorance breeds fear

Emotional dangers
The young child:
1   Cannot express himself clearly.
2   Is not yet adaptable.
3   Lives in the present and cannot understand 'tomorrow'.
4   Has a lively imagination and makes simple things seen or heard into frightening fantasies.
5   Is very dependant upon mother.
Some *reactions* that children show when in hospital:
1   Undue crying and refusing to be comforted.
2   Regressing – bed-wetting, thumb sucking.
3   Exceptionally good behaviour.
4   Withdrawal and turning away from parents when they visit.

Teach your child about hospital through play and books
Teddy demonstration. Special sleep. Giving Teddy a pretend anaesthetic.

The role of the parent
Parents should remember always to be *truthful*.

If it is going to hurt, say so. Never use the doctors and nurses as a threat. Remember to tell the staff if the child is used to going to bed as a punishment.

EXAMPLE

A student recalls vividly her stay in hospital:

My stay in hospital
I was about five when I had to go into the children's hospital to have my adenoids out.

Everyone told me it was really good going into hospital. They said that you have ice-cream and jelly everyday. I don't think I knew what I was really having done because I didn't really understand.

I wasn't nervous about going in because they kept telling me it was good.

My Mum's neighbour's daughter gave me her doll and blanket to take with me because she knew I liked it.

The day I was going I felt unsure of everything, but I didn't really worry.

When I got to the hospital my Mum, Dad and I waited in the waiting room. A nurse came and she put a plastic bracelet name tag on my wrist. She took me into a room where I was weighed and examined. After that my Mum put my things into my bed cabinet and she left and said she would be back later. I didn't get upset and worried. Some of the children were playing and I thought I was at another little school and that I had changed my other school.

In my ward was one girl and all the rest were boys. She was in the opposite row of beds. She had long black hair and quite a dark colour of skin. I can't remember her name.

Later that afternoon we had our tea at our little tables and chairs. I can remember what we had. We had boiled potatoes, beef in gravy and peas and carrots and for pudding ice-cream and jelly like they said.

Afterwards we had to get washed and undressed and go and see the doctor. When it was my turn he said when I go to bed that I had to take my vest off. He gave me a tiny little cup with some white liquid inside and I had to drink it and it was horrible. I dreaded drinking that every day.

I went back to my ward and made friends with the girl. She didn't have to take her vest off but some of the boys did. I didn't want to because I thought it was rude and I didn't want any nurses to come and look at me.

Later that evening my Mum and Dad came up and I was very happy. They brought me up some sweets and I ate them secretly because my Mum's neighbour said you have to share them and I didn't think I would get many.

Another little boy younger than me came into the ward and was put into a cot at the end. He didn't stop crying all night.

When my Mum and Dad went they told me to be good and that they would give me a surprise when I came out.

When we all went to bed the little boy was still crying. I took my doll to bed and I made sure the nurses didn't see my neck.

I could see into the next ward and I could see other children reading in bed. I classed them as really old children but they weren't really. I thought they must be older than me. I didn't feel like going to sleep so I just looked around me. By this time the little boy had stopped crying and had fallen asleep. Everybody else was asleep but not me. I saw the nurse coming so I pretended to be asleep. She took my doll out and put her on the cabinet and then she went. I put her back and said to myself 'horrible old nurse'.

The next day the girl and I sat on her bed doing puzzles and reading comics which a fat nurse brought into us.

At dinner time we never had any dinner only that white stuff. My Mum and Dad came up and said my Nan and Grandad are outside and that they were coming in. I felt really happy.

My Mum and Dad went out to get them and they were a long time and I got upset and tears kept coming into my eyes. I kept wiping them quickly so that the nurse didn't see me, and my Mum and Dad, Nan and Grandad wouldn't notice. I thought I was a big girl.

When they did come back I turned against my Mum and Dad because they had left me on my own and I thought they were not coming back. I went to my Nan and Grandad for love at that time but I soon got over it. I told them I hadn't had any dinner and that I was hungry. They didn't say much and didn't tell me I was going to have an operation.

We didn't have an evening meal either. I was starving.

The little boy cried every time his Mum and Dad came and went.

I can remember faintly waking up in the operation room and seeing a woman looking down on me and closing my eyes, and that was it.

At five in the morning I woke and there were cups and straws on my cabinet. The nurse came over and gave me some lemon to drink, but I couldn't suck at first and I got really frightened. Then the nurse bent the straw and I could drink.

That day we were all moved into the next ward.

That tea-time it was cheese on toast with tomatoes. I didn't like it so I thought they would starve me, but they didn't' I had some rice pudding which was lumpy. I had to take that white stuff again which tasted worse.

The next morning I was dying to go to the toilet, but there was no nurse in my ward to tell her. There was a bell on the wall but I was too frightened to ring it.

I got my towel out of my cabinet and put it on my bed and sat on it and went to the toilet. I had the towel back in the cabinet before the nurse came back. I felt relieved afterwards.

The next day I was to go home. I had a bath which my Mum gave me.

My friend didn't go home the same day, she had to stay a couple more days. I said good-bye to her and her dad and she looked very sad.

On the way home in the car we stopped at a toy shop and my Mum and Dad bought me a purse, a bag and a draught set. I was really pleased.

When I did get home my Mum's neighbour was waiting for me and she had been knitting me a cardigan. It was lovely and it was turquoise.

I kept wishing I could go back again because I liked it. I still wish the same thing.

As a student in this course, the same girl went to hospital to visit the child who was the object of her Child Study.

My visit to the hospital to see Craig

Craig is two years old. He was put in hospital because he was scalded by boiling water from a kettle. He had climbed up on a chair and tipped the hot water over him.

His Mum and I came in and he was making trains with stickle bricks. He was very happy to see Mum but turned away from her when she wanted to play and hold him. He kept hitting Mum and cried and screamed and wouldn't go to Mum or me, only the staff.

He cried when a nurse looked at his burns on his chest.

He didn't want his teeth cleaned so he struggled.

A nurse gave him a biscuit and he quietened down.

The nurse explained to Craig's Mum that he was punishing her. Craig's Mum was very upset.

We showed Craig the musical rocking chair and he was pleased and he sat and rocked in it. He played with cars and a garage and the train with the animals in it.

When dinner time came he was really overwhelmed to see the staff bring the trolleys in. His eyes lit up and you could see he was hungry and he cried because his dinner wasn't put on the plate at once, so the staff dished his dinner up first. It was shepherds pie and vegetables. He sat at the table and his Mum wanted to cut some of his food up but he wouldn't let her. He kept bashing his spoon in his dinner. He ate all his dinner and drank two full cups of lemon straight down and afterwards ate his jelly and ice-cream and he drank another half cup of orange. When he went back into the ward he ate an apple.

His Nan came up and he was pleased to see her. She played with him and later he helped the nurse wash the plastic bed lining and then he played with another little boy called Russell who was two and a half. They played with the helicopters. Later in the afternoon he went in the playroom and looked out of the window at the park. Then Craig and Russell got the trolley of bricks and played with them.

I, his Mum and his Nan, had to creep out and go home otherwise he would have cried and not wanted us to go. His Mum did not stay with him because she had to look after the other children.

What have I learned?   Questions on preparing children for going to hospital
1   Why should *all* children be prepared for hospital?
2   (a) What methods can a parent use to familiarise a child with aspects of hospital life?
(b) What kind of words must the child understand fully?
3   How should a parent prepare the child for any shock or pain they may receive?
4   From this chapter give some examples of cruelty in the treatment of children by hospital or parents who meant well. What was the mistake the parents made? What was the mistake the hospital made?
5   What sort of visits help the child most?
6   Why is a noisy protest about going to hospital by the child said to be preferrable to sullen acquiescence?
7   Say why small frequent gifts will help the child more than a few expensive ones?
8   What does 'regress' mean?
9   What positive things can come from a hospital visit? (apart from healing).

A task to complete as a group (three or four students)
Read through the 'My Stay in Hospital' and 'My Visit to the Hospital to see Craig'. Decide what you think were the good things that the parents, family and hospital did to help the child in each case, describe any ways in which things could have been done differently as suggested in the chapter.

List signs of stress shown by the child patients and signs that they were content.

The Six to Seven year olds: development guide

Before the age of five, the child's progress has been governed primarily by his physical development, ie the *ability* to do things.

Between five and seven the child is influenced more by external social influences. There are no major changes in physical development – the child grows taller, and is usually thinner. Good diet, 11–12 hours of sleep and fresh air are all important.

Behaviour
The child at school learns to conform to the group, and is fairly co-operative. Adult authority is accepted but the child still has to learn practical skills to adapt socially.

Social behaviour
'Herd instinct'. The child has a strong urge to belong to the group and be accepted by it. Will go to any lengths to belong. Copy friends in dress, mannerisms, speech. They like their clothes to be similar to others. Boys join in wrestling and violent games even if it distresses them. They hate to be different from others in their group.

Practical competence: Learning 'how to do'.
The child once he has started school is under pressure to learn how to do certain things – especially to read, write and do sums.

To be able to learn these skills the child must be able to concentrate. But to be *able* to concentrate the child must feel secure, happy and confident.

Children who start school (or playgroup) before the age of five, are on the whole, still ahead of the others at seven. They learn to adjust to the group early, and are more ready for the formal learning.

Obviously, children who are unhappy or worried have difficulty concentrating and therefore have difficulty learning.

Increasing skills:
At school through:
PE
Music and movement
Games and swimming

Also increasingly skilful with hands:
Drawing and painting
Writing

In the playground: through their
love to practise skills, eg skipping
hopscotch
hand games – clapping
                    cat's craddle
   The child's memory increases and games with songs and rhymes are enjoyed.

Vision, speech and hearing
A medical is given to children during their first year at school. Heart, lungs, feet, height and weight, are checked.
There are routine dental inspections.
Sight is tested.
Hearing is tested.
   Dental disease is very common. English children have the worst teeth in Europe. They also consume the most sugar, sweets, squash, fizzy drinks. During this stage they begin to loose their 'milk teeth'.

Imperfect sight
Often poor progress at school is due to poor vision. Easily detected and treated. Test also done for colour blindness.

Speech
A child should speak clearly at this age. Speech difficulties, such as a stammer or lisp, can be a social handicap if the child is teased at school. Speech therapy is available.

Hearing
A child has problems learning in class if hearing is defective. Can also be dangerous – particularly crossing roads.

Problems
Stammering
Soiling
Bed-wetting
Stealing
Undue aggression
Over-activity
Shyness and withdrawal

   Children need extra help with all these problems. Insecure children may try to buy friends with sweets or money or constantly boast and brag.

Factors which affect the child's achievements at school

These are *generalisations* from a survey of children up to the age of seven.

Family size: children from small families (one or two children) did better with reading than those from large families (four or more). Presumably parents had more time to spend and there were less distractions.

Working mothers: small difference. Children were slightly better readers if mothers did not work. No effect on social adjustments if the mother has started working before the child started school. Slightly bad effect if she started working *after* the child started school. Probably because proper arrangements would be made for a pre-school child while the mother worked. A school might not have any proper arrangements made for after school, or when ill.

Parents' Involvement in education: children whose parents took an interest in school and actively participated in children's activities generally did better than children whose parents showed no concern.

What have I learned? Questions on development of children from five to seven

1 What physical changes, if any, will occur between the ages of five and seven?

2 What does the author say is needed to maintain healthy physical development at this age?

3 Say what the child's attitude to adult authority is at this age?

4 The author says that boys join in wrestling and violent games even if it distresses them. Why do you think they do this?

5 What evidence is there that it is good for children to start school or playgroups before the age of five?

6 Why should the child starting school particularly need to be happy and confident?

7 Can you describe some of the skills playground games might develop?

8 The author mentioned five school subjects important to this age group. What skills do you think they would develop?

9 Why should games with songs and rhymes be particularly enjoyed at this age?

10 What reason does the author suggest why English children have the worst teeth in Europe?

11 Why is this the age chosen for so many medical tests?

12 What particular difficulties does the child encounter if speech difficulties are not tackled?

13 The author lists a series of problems on page ooo. What sort of things would cause these problems do you think? (Discuss this question in small groups.)

14 Put into your own words details of the factors which affect the child's achievement at this age.

15 Why is the adult urged to read to the child of this age books which have language and ideas too complex for the child to handle? What advantage is suggested?

16   The author underlines and emphasises some key points of importance
about the reading of children of this age. Write several sentences explaining the
importance of each one with examples, if necessary.
Fantasy
Ethical concepts
Fact and fiction
Self-identification
Vocabulary enlargement.

The untruths children tell

Untruth: good fantasy

Children of this age are unable to distinguish between fantasy and reality as this
is, to a large extent, acquired through experience. As adults we conspire to
confuse them further with stories of Father Christmas, the Tooth Fairy,
gooseberry bush babies, etc. These myths give the child a sense of awe and
wonder, stimulating the imagination which helps them develop sensitivity
towards others.

Untruth: bad fantasy

Just as children believe these myths absolutely, so they will be genuinely
terrified of the Bogeyman, the Tiger under the bed or the Witch at the window.
When the adult's attempts to reassure the child by denying the existance of
these monsters fail, the adult becomes impatient with the child for refusing to
accept their rationale that because they cannot be seen, they do not exist. The
fear can usually be exorcized only through a ritual involving the cause of the
fear, eg entice the Tiger to leave with a bowl of milk! Drawing or painting the
subject of the fear is a common way of giving the child control over the thing he
fears.

Untruth: fear

Children will deny their misdemeanours sometimes very vehemently, even if
the adult witnessed it. The adult may find this threatening and perplexing. The
reasons are complex and have to do with the child's fear of consequences – real
or imagined or unimaginable. One child recalls smashing a greenhouse roof
with a ball and his frantic denial because of his fear of the unknown
consequences. A parent warned a recalcitrant child 'if you don't get out of the
bath I will pull the plug out and you will go down the plug hole'. The child
accepted the statement literally and became extremely fearful every time the
plug was pulled out of his bath for a very long time afterwards. If a bathful of
water was able to vanish down the plug hole he had no difficulty in imagining
his own disappearance.

By denying the truth a child may hope to avoid the withdrawal of love and
approval which is sometimes used as a punishment. Faced with such a situation
the adult can articulate for the child what they are both feeling, explain the

actual, as opposed to the imagined, consequences. For example, if a child breaks a precious ornament and denies having done it the adult's response should be to explain to the child that he lies because he fears his parents may cease to love him, or hurt him severely for what he has done. The next step is to explain what is to happen: for the child to help clear up the mess and perhaps make a contribution to the cost out of pocket money or make reparation by performing a good deed. The adult should also acknowledge his distress at the loss of a prized possession but assure the child that he is loved.

Untruth: attempt to hurt someone

This occurs more often than not when a child feels rejected or jealous. Such feelings usually leave the child with a sense of confusion or guilt. The object may be alienate the parents, teacher or friends, affection from a sibling or to land someone in trouble because the child envies their talents, good looks, attention received or material possessions. These untruths may be used to break friendships between children where the child feels left out. In a certain class of six year olds one girl was in the enviable position of always appearing in beautiful clothes with a doting mother to pick her up and sweep her away in a large and comfortable car at the end of the school day. A deprived child in the class found this too much one day when the girl turned up with a beautiful set of felts to complete some work the class were engaged in. During playtime she went back to the classroom and scribbled all over the girl's work and when class returned, told the teacher that she had seen the girl spoil her own work. Fortunately the teacher realised what had happened and why. She dealt with the matter by explaining to the culprit why she had done it, thus acknowledging her feelings, gave her her own felts to work with, and set her a task to do for the benefit of the class.

The essential thing for the adult to put right is not only the consequences of the untruth and make the miscreant put things right, but also to attempt to deal with the original hurt which led to the untruth, as the teacher did in the above example.

'There are no sinners only sin' said D.H. Lawrence, and as adults we have the difficult task of making children aware of the sin without feeling irrevocably a sinner.

Untruth: exaggeration

Exaggeration is used by a child to enhance the importance of what the child is saying and so ensure an impact on the adult or other children. A boy came home from his first day at school wanting to share his experience of being a member of a group as large as his class. 'There are loads of children in my class,' he began by saying. 'Surely not that many', his mother corrected him. The boy responded by saying that there were 50 in the class. He recalled that he chose that number because it seemed to him a large and impressive figure.

Another example is when a rather shy girl, from a large family, whose only friend had a fall in the playground and grazed her knee. She played the important role of accompanying her friend to the Head's office so that the knee could be attended to. Important though that was to her and gave her stature, she realised it would be small fry when retold to her family. She therefore told her family that her friend had a deep cut which needed stitches and that she had accompanied her to hospital in the ambulance. Next day meeting in the playground she found the mother offering sympathy to the other girl's mother, the untruth was revealed to the mother's annoyance and embarrassment, this she in no uncertain terms communicated to her daughter.

Untruth: bragging
Bragging arises out of feelings of inadequacy. A child may be in a deprived situation, may feel unable to keep up with others or on the other hand have surplus of material goods but feel insecure emotionally and socially.

A boy whose father was in hospital paralysed after a car crash had to move to another house and start a new school. He was unable to cope with telling his new classmates the truth and invented an exciting absent racing driver father.

A class was asked to bring games to play on the last day of term. One girl realised that the only possibility was an old snakes and ladders game. Hearing her friends discussing all the exciting games they were going to bring – she pretended she had a marvellous new game which she had seen advertised on the television. Next day when she brought her old game in, her classmates laughed and she burst into tears. Fortunately, the teacher realised what had happened and after diverting the other children took the girl aside, talked to her, calmed her down and comforted her. She then showed an interest in the game and soon had a whole group of children playing it happily. As a result the girl felt proud and accepted.

Adults encourage white lies to avoid hurting feelings and social upset. For instance encouraging a child at a party to pretend to be full-up rather than admit disliking food offered. However, this concept of white lies is very confusing to a child of this age who is struggling to grasp the difference between reality and fantasy and who is told that truth is good and lies are bad.

Notes on the reasons children tell untruths: an aid for work guide
Fantasy (good) eg Father Christmas, Tooth Fairy.
Adults introduce children to the idea of fantasy in the form of Father Christmas, tooth fairy, fairy stories. They do this to make life more interesting and exciting.
Fantasy (bad), eg Bogey man, Witches, Monsters.
Children do not have enough experience of the world to know what is real and what is imagined; they are very gullible, adults use this to inspire awe and as a form of control, eg if you are not good the bogey man will get you. To the child fantasy figures that adults introduce them to as well as ones they imagine become a *total reality*.
Fear, eg I didn't do it, it wasn't me, it was the cat, the canary, the baby, the teddy – *it wasn't me*.
Children deny that they have done something wrong, broken a favourite

ornament, stolen something even if they have been seen doing it because they are afraid of the consequences:

Real

Threatened

Imagined

Losing parental love and approval.

To hurt someone: when a child tells a deliberate untruth to get someone into trouble: usually done through feelings of jealousy.

Exaggeration: children live in a world of competent, knowing adults. To communicate an experience or a feeling the children enlarge in order to create an impact.

Bragging: a child when he feels inadequate will show off about something he hasn't got or make it bigger than it is. Sometimes they do it because they haven't learned to take other people's feelings into account and 'show off' about things they possess eg 'My Daddy has the biggest car'.

White lies: children are instructed to tell white lies in order to save people's feelings or get out of an awkward situation, 'Don't tell your friend you have already had one of these for your birthday'.

How to deal with the child

Acknowledge the child's feelings, and tell him what the consequences will be. For example:

Get him to clear up the mess he has made

Help with the chores

Don't give him as much pocket money.

Make sure the consequences are not too awful!

Untruths work guide

Recalling a time we told an untruth or someone else we know has, illuminates our own motivation and gives us the ability to understand the same behaviour in other people: children as well as adults. There are indeed many adults who find it difficult to tell the truth because, as children, they had not been helped to come to terms with difficult emotions, such as jealousy, or feelings of inadequacy, and so as adults continue to resort to 'childish behaviour'. The youngest in the family is often the one who as an adult is prone to exaggeration!

Using the following paragraph headings *analyse examples of different kinds of untruths* that you told or someone you know well has. *Read the examples quoted first.* They should reassure you that other people follow some patterns of behaviour. *Refer to the notes* about the different categories of untruths before you write.

Explain briefly the category of untruth you are going to write about

Give relevant information about the child, eg age, position in the family, any experience the child has had that would have influenced what you are going to write about.

Describe the incident, eg what happened, were there any rituals involved?

Write about what motivated you, eg what you did, what you believed and what it was that influenced you.

Describe your feelings.

Write about the adult's reaction.

Give an informed comment.

EXAMPLE

THE REASONS WHY CHILDREN TELL UNTRUTHS

Good Fantasy – Father Christmas and Fairies

Good fantasies give the child a sense of awe and wonder, and stimulates the imagination.

The incident

The fantasy that I remember most was that of Father Christmas and his helpers. His little helpers were Swiss pixies and fairies. I was told by my parents and my older brothers and sisters that on Christmas Eve Father Christmas had to deliver all the presents to the good children at their houses, and if you had been naughty then you wouldn't get any presents. So when it came to about a week before Christmas I would behave really well, and try to help my Mum do the housework and try to be nice to my brothers and sisters.

When I asked my brother and sisters how Father Christmas managed to get to all of the children's houses and deliver the presents in one evening, they said that he had lots of helpers, who posted all of the presents down the chimney and collected any food that children left for him. They told me that Father Christmas flew from house to house on a sleigh with four reindeer pulling it. All the presents were stocked on the back in two large sacks, one for girls and one for boys.

Motivation

When my family told me these stories about Father Christmas I really did believe them, because I think I was a bit lonely at the time as my brothers and sisters were older and went out with their friends, and my Mum had my little sister to look after who was only a baby. I remember crying a lot and my Mum asking me what was wrong. I told her that at school I had spilt some water over the floor, and now Father Christmas wouldn't bring me any presents. So my Mum told me that if I wrote a letter to Father Christmas saying sorry, and gave it to her, so she could put it in the open fire, he would still bring some presents. So I wrote a letter and it was sent up the chimney to him. And I was really pleased when I woke up on Christmas Day and I had lots of presents at the bottom of my bed.

My feelings

One thing I know is that Father Christmas was very real to me and I truly believed all of the many stories that I was told. And I remember telling my little sister when she was about five the stories I had been told as a child. And she believed them all too.

Adult reaction

My Mum and Dad always told me stories about Father Christmas and the Tooth Fairy but what I could not understand as a child was that sometimes my Mum would tell my brothers and sisters to stop when they were telling me stories, and she would try and make me understand that Father Christmas didn't really exist. At first when she told me this I started to cry and wouldn't listen to her, but in the end I accepted the fact that Father Christmas didn't really exist.

My comment

I think I would tell my children stories for a while and try to make them believe in Father Christmas, because it makes Christmas much more exciting for them.

Bad fantasy

Bad fantasies make children frightened and scared and have nightmares.
I was five years old and when it came to bed time this is when I was scared of the Sandman.

The incident

One morning when I woke up and rubbed my eyes to get the sleep away I started to think about it. I asked my Dad how it gets there and who puts it there. My father replied the 'Sandman'. 'Who's he?'
'He is a man who carries a big sack of sand around with him, and when everybody is asleep he sprinkles a bit into their eyes.' That night when I went to bed I lay awake for this man. Who was he? I was really scared because now I knew who he was I thought he was going to throw too much sand and blind me. I couldn't go to sleep any more. One night my Mum and Dad asked me what was wrong. I told them and they told me if I went to sleep and closed my eyes then he wouldn't be able to get so much in. So I did and this made me overcome my bad fantasy.

The feelings

I felt terrible and scared but once my Mum and Dad had told me to close my eyes I felt better. I was most scared of being blinded by it and never be able to see again.

Adult reaction

The adults did very well because they made me feel very relaxed.

My comment

I'm very glad I got over this because being scared of losing your sight is like realising how people feel who are already blind.

FEAR

The reasons why children tell untruths

Children tell untruths because of fear, when they are afraid, because of the consequences whether real or imagined.

The incident

My sister Victoria is four years old, nearly five. This is an age where children can be very clumsy. Well I was looking after her the other day. We were having a little argument because she wouldn't do something I asked her to do. Then in her temper she threw her cup of water in the air and all the water went down the back of the television. All of a sudden she burst out crying. When I asked her what was the matter, she said 'Don't tell Mummy I did it, will you?'

I told her that Mum would be ever so cross because she had damaged the television; lucky it wasn't on, it would have blown up. But all she kept saying was 'please don't tell'. I said to her, 'I'm going to have to, if she turns it on it will blow up'. She replied 'Tell her some water fell down there'.

She was really pleading with me as if she was so frightened at what my Mum was going to do.

When my Mum came in, I had to tell her. She smacked Victoria and told her off, and Victoria pleaded saying 'I didn't do it honest, it fell in there'. She swore blind she never did it, and one time she said I did it.

What motivated the child to do it

Victoria didn't realise the harm she would do. She just lost her temper and threw the thing nearest to her. She has probably got this temper from one of us, and seen us throw things about in temper. She lied because she wanted to just put the blame on someone else. She was afraid to own up that she did it.

How the child felt

Victoria must have felt very afraid by the way she was acting, the way she was shaking. She also knew what was going to happen when Mum got home. She knew she would be cross, and I felt rotten because she was pleading with me to stick up for her but there was no way I could. She knew that Mum wouldn't believe her so she told her it just fell in. Her mind doesn't think like an adult. To Vicky that was a perfectly good explanation she gave, so she was confused by the response she got.

The adults reaction
My mother's reaction was to smack Vicky and punish her, but it wasn't as if Vicky had done it on purpose. It was an accident. Vicky meant to throw the water but not down the back of the television.

My comment
I think that my mother could have punished Vicky in a less severe way. She could have understood how frightened Vicky was at the time. Also she could have understood why Victoria was lying which was because she was frightened so she tried to take the blame off herself.

TO HURT SOMEONE

This is when a child, or older person, tells an untruth to hurt someone deliberately or to get someone into trouble.

The incident
The incident I remember happened when I was very little and involved my sister and me. I can't remember exactly how old I was, but my sister is two years older than me. My Mum was doing some cooking and said that Lucy could help her but I couldn't because it was too difficult for me to understand, and there was a lot of using the cooker involved. I just sat and watched, feeling very angry that my sister was cooking and I wasn't.

I thought it was very unfair. I heard my Mum say to my sister several times *not* to touch the knobs controlling the cooker flame, and then the phone rang and my Mum had to go and answer it. My sister was busy doing something with her back to me, so I quickly jumped off my chair and went over to the cooker and, pretending to look at the food in one of the saucepans, I turned the heat right up underneath it. I moved away from the cooker and watched the water boil over the top, then I went into the room where my Mum was on the phone and told her Lucy had turned the gas up. My Mum went running into the kitchen and I went upstairs quickly.

The motivation
I think what motivated me to behave in this way was because I was very jealous of my sister doing something grown up, like cooking, and me having nothing to do. I think I wanted my sister's company and I felt left out and lonely.

My feelings
Before the incident I felt envious and very angry. When I turned the heat up I felt very excited when I went upstairs, I think I felt 'mixed up' about what I had done but when I got upstairs I didn't really think I had done anything wrong. I just sat and waited for my sister.

Adult's reaction and the effect on me

First of all my Mum was very angry and shouted at my sister and sent her out of the kitchen because what she had done had been dangerous. When my sister came into our room she was upset and didn't want to play anyway, so I was left how I was in the first place. I think my Mum then realised that it had been me who had done it, and she became very angry with me. My sister was allowed to go back to the kitchen and I had to stay in our room on my own. I felt very ashamed.

My comment

I think my Mum dealt with the situation in the wrong way. She didn't see why I had done it (for attention) she could only see that I had told a deliberate nasty lie and also done something very dangerous. But if I had been involved in the first place it would never have happened.

BRAGGING

Bragging arises out of feelings of inadequacy.

The incident

When I was six years old I was staying with my Nan. I was very independent and loved boasting about things because my friends always would be one above me. So I got them back by telling an untruth.

My auntie worked in the NAFFI with the Queen's Guards. One day I went to meet her from work with my Nan and Grandad. I met one of the Queen's Guards and spoke to him. When I went to school I told all my friends that I had met the Queen and had dinner with her. All my friends thought this was good except one little boy who was doubtful about this. So when my Mum came to meet me from school the little boy asked my Mum, and my Mum immediately said, 'No, where did you get that idea from'. Ever since that day that same boy has never spoken to me.

The motivation

I did this because I didn't like everyone being one above me. When I go to school I have no stories to tell my friends but they would tell me theirs.

My feelings

I felt very ashamed of myself and I didn't want to go to school ever again. My friends would tease me.

Adult reaction

My Mum reacted very strongly and she put mustard on my tongue. She said to me if I ever did that again she would cut my tongue out.

My comment

I realise now that I shouldn't have done it, and when I said it I felt ashamed of myself, but I also felt unhappy. Children brag about things like this because they either want attention or they don't like being left out.

WHITE LIES

We teach children to tell white lies, maybe to save somebody's feelings – as a form of good manners.

The incident
The incident I remember was at Christmas time. It involves my sister. We always had lots of relatives over to see us and my Grandparents were staying with us. My sister was six years old and I was four. When my Auntie gave my sister her Christmas present my Mum noticed that the shape was the same as the present that my Grandpa had given my sister. As my sister started to unwrap it my Mum realised it was the same, quickly she took my sister's hand and asked her to help with the tea. When my Mum was in the kitchen with my sister she explained to her that the present was the same, but that she must pretend that it wasn't and thank Auntie Sue very much for the present. When my sister finished unwrapping the present she said thank you and gave my Auntie a kiss, but she was very quiet.

The motivation
Obviously my sister was motivated to behave the way she did entirely because my Mum told her to. It was very unnatural for my sister.

Child's feelings
My sister was, of course, very excited about opening all her presents. Then after what my Mum did Lucy became very confused and didn't understand what she was doing or why. After she had thanked Auntie Sue Lucy became very quiet and sat looking very puzzled for a while.

The adult reaction
My Mum's reaction when she saw that the presents were the same was almost panic. She didn't want to hurt anyone's feelings and so she acted in the way she thought necessary. She tried to explain to my sister why she had to tell a white lie but my sister couldn't understand she had always been told that lying was wrong.

My comment
I think my Mum acted in the wrong way. It wouldn't have really mattered if Lucy had said she had a present like that already. Lucy might not have even remembered that she already had one. What my Mum did only served to bewilder and confuse my sister.

Children and television

Young children believe everything they see on television because they don't have enough experience to tell what is real and what is a figment of someone's imagination. The Daleks in *Dr Who* exist, Superman can really fly, children believe in these and other phenomena in the same way they believe that Father Christmas rides through the night on Christmas Eve in a sleigh drawn by reindeer and delivers presents to all good children. I remember when I was a small child lying awake full of anxiety worrying how Father Christmas would know where to bring my present; this was in war-torn Europe, my family and I had been deported to Siberia. That fact was of less consequence to me than the reality of my belief in that magic person. He did know where to bring my gift: my mother and sister understanding my anxiety, unravelled a jumper and from the wool made up two figures to represent Hansel and Gretel. I found them in my slipper, as is the custom there, and that all important part of my world remained intact.

Children's television programmes in this country are reputed to be among the best in the world, and without doubt many programmes enhance the child's knowledge about the world, excite his imagination, introduce him to new ideas and make a child's life all the richer by its contributions. Such programmes are carefully prepared by experts for children. Unfortunately those are not the only television programmes that children watch. Many children also watch programmes intended for adult viewing and there is no doubt that the children who frequently watch adult television have more anxieties and worries, sleep less well because they are disturbed by bad dreams; they are tired, less alert and are less able to concentrate and learn at school.

Some adults regard television as a means of keeping children quiet, and use it as a substitute for organised activities, such as flying a kite on a windy afternoon, baking with the children, making opportunities for messy play, playing board games, taking them out for a walk – giving them lots of opportunity for physical play which uses up energy, puts them in a good mood, gives them a healthy appetite and exercises their bodies. Adults and children miss so much if the children are left to stay up and watch adult television at the end of each day instead of the adult spending what should be regarded as special time putting the children to bed, talking to them, playing with them in the bath, reading them a favourite story.

Children often are left to watch television on their own and of course, occasionally this does no harm but if it happens too often, viewing potential is lost. The child has no one to interpret for him things he sees and doesn't understand, he can't ask questions, share impressions, there is no one to focus his viewing on interesting points or extend what he sees with other experiences. The viewing can become a solitary, passive and sometimes even frightening experience for the child.

The horrific influence of some video nasties, particularly on young people who are mentally not very bright, has been brought to our notice in the newspapers reporting on awful crimes committed after such people watched 'horror movies'.

If young children are allowed to watch all aspects of adult life before they understand them, serious repercussions could follow. This was particularly brought home to me when my son – then two and a half years old – threw a stone at a passing car as he was standing by our garden gate. I was horrified to discover that he was not so much concerned about the telling off he received, as disappointed that his action had not caused the car to explode 'as in Northern Ireland', he explained. He had been watching the early evening news before being taken up to bed.

We really ought to know what children are going to watch on television. I once suggested to my 13 year old son that he might like to watch *I Claudius* which was being shown on BBC 2. A simple tale, I mistakenly thought, about the Roman Empire. As the story unfolded, I realised the mistake I had made. All that was twisted and corrupt was being presented in full technicolour detail – everything from incest to orgy. I explained to my son that the programmes were unsuitable because he had not the experience of life to be able to put the view of adult sexuality portrayed in *I Claudius* into perspective, and that I didn't want his view of love and sex to be distorted by it. He helped me out with a simple but effective maxim: 'It's like getting Christmas presents in the summer'.

Exposing young minds to images they do not yet comprehend will result in the child's imagination and sensibilities being blunted and his perception of the world distorted.

Young children should watch only children's programmes and the television set should not come between them and their legitimate activities. Adults should watch with the child, at least some of the time, participating and sharing in the experience; and choosing what programmes to watch can be a useful learning opportunity in decision-making. Babies' central nervous systems can be disturbed if they watch the screen for any length of time and this can affect their concentration later on. One small girl was told by her mother that if she continued to watch television as much she would get square eyes. She believed her mother implicitly and from then on wouldn't go into the sitting room when the set was on. It is a pity there is not some tangible evidence of the harm unrestricted viewing can cause.

Children in Special Circumstances

I don't remember what I did but my Mum told me that when I was little I was jumping on my new bed, when I had been told not to, and I fell off and bruised my legs very badly. When I went to school in PE I was asked how I had done it and instead of being told off about jumping on my bed I said that my Dad had hit me. Straight away the welfare people came to my house because it was at the time when Maria Collwell had been battered to death and they were checking up on anything like that. Eventually everything was sorted out and I got told off for lying and also for jumping on my bed.

Children in special circumstances

I asked a student why she had not handed in a piece of work. She tossed her head and accused me of picking on her. I pointed out that everyone else in the group had completed the work and so why hadn't she – 'I come from a single parent family!' was the answer she gave me. There were several other students in that group who also came from single parent families, some who were struggling with coming to terms with step parents, and others who were still smarting from the hurt caused by their parents' divorce: others who were coping with bitter rows at home and some, no doubt, whose 'special circumstances' I knew nothing about. In a sense each one of us encounters difficulties in our lives which alter the way we feel and see ourselves in relation to other people and influence the way we behave.

Special circumstances can influence what happens to millions of children – or a mere handful. A physical handicap is visible and people will make allowances, but an emotional scar gives no physical manifestation, yet can cause devastating havoc in a person's ability to make relationships and lead a happy and fulfilled life. In this last section of the book I want to look at some of these special circumstances. Because the subjects are painful and can cause hurt, some sections I have chosen to present in an analytical and factual way.

For this reason also I have used a different approach for the work to be done by the students in this section.
I have found it helpful to introduce each aspect by inviting an expert to talk to the class, eg

Representative from the NSPCC
Experienced Foster Mother
Warden of a Children's Home
Someone with experience of handicapped children.

Ideas for follow up to this study could be imaginative work based on the knowledge acquired, which could take a variety of forms.

Divorced parents

Children often blame themselves for things that go wrong in the family – if only I had been 'good' it wouldn't have happened. They are too young to be able to articulate those thoughts and feelings and they may well linger with them into adulthood. Often a child feels that divorce is somehow his own fault, they seek constant punishment because of an unconscious sense of guilt. A death in the family can have the same effect. Misguided adults assume that because a child stops talking about a mother who has died, or a father who has left home, they have forgotten them. That is not so. Adults should talk openly about the problems to the child and articulate for them how they are feeling and show acceptance of those feelings. When the adult is open with the child he will feel more secure and more able to face the problems. It's going to hurt, it's going to be upsetting to move home, to split possessions. They will find it difficult to concentrate on sums when they are worrying whether Mum will leave too, when Dad has left home.

Children at times of stress often regress and become much more childish, wet their bed, become clingy and whiny – all very difficult for the adults to handle with patience and understanding when they have their own pressures to cope with. One Mum asked in bewilderment, 'Why are they being so naughty now that their Dad has left – why are they punishing *me* for his desertion?' Another found it difficult to understand how her reliable and sensible eight year old refused to go to school, clung to her, wet his bed and even started to baby talk. 'I was expecting to be able to rely on him at least', she wailed.

It is a great temptation to try to get the child to take sides against one or other of the parents and this must be avoided, however high the feelings run. The child will cope much better if he is allowed to continue his relationship with both parents. Directly divorce has been mooted, the school should be informed as they can play their part in helping the family.

The question of access to the child very often causes severe tension between the divorced parents, but until the conflict is resolved the child will face grave unhappiness.

The following extract, written by a 16 year old student about the reaction of her four year old sister to a very unhappy situation at home, clearly defines the effects of the trauma on the child's behaviour.

EXAMPLES

Difficulties

At the moment Victoria is very difficult to handle. This is because she is very unstable. There are a lot of things going on around her she doesn't understand.

At home our Mum and Dad aren't getting on too well at the moment, but I, being older can understand. Vicky is living in an environment of constant rowing and arguing.

I notice how Vicky's behaviour has changed a lot because of this. She sleeps with my Mum and won't go to bed until my Mum does, or if she is put to bed she comes down and says she can't sleep. This is because I supposed she's worried that something may happen to my Mum. Also she is very clinging to my Mum because sometimes if my Mum doesn't want to cuddle Vicky she will reject her and say, she doesn't want Vicky because she is a horrible girl! This makes Vicky worse, so in a case like this I try to comfort Vicky.

Vicky is also very close to me because I always take her out, do things with her, and generally I am with her more than my Mum is, whereas Vicky is not close to my Dad because my Mum turns Vicky away from him.

Also my Mum spoils Vicky, which is not a good thing because Vicky needs love from my Mum, not from things my Mum buys her. I suppose it's like saying 'My Mum buys Vicky's love'.

Although Vicky outwardly seems very happy, energetic and lively, she is also very *hurt* deep down.

Vicky knows that my Dad is going to move away to another house, but she doesn't understand, and when my Mum speaks to Vicky she sometimes says the wrong things. She tells Vicky that 'Daddy's a horrible man, he's going to live with another woman'. That is no way to speak to a five-year-old.

When Victoria is older I hope she will improve. She has just gone into a new class, and today the first day back, she has been sent to the headmistresses office because she is being spiteful. This behaviour may well be connected with the circumstances.

DISOBEDIENT BEHAVIOUR (LORRAINE)

The child

At the time of the incident, I was nine years old. There are only my sister and me in the family, I being the youngest. There is two years difference between us. I would consider myself fairly shy, but on knowing somebody I become very chatty. I am not deliberately naughty, without a cause. I am jealous of my sister, when she has something that I want.

The actual incident

It began by my Dad, sister and I taking presents to my Mum's friend at Easter. After a while my Dad left, leaving us behind. Knowing that something was wrong, as we were made to stay upstairs and play, we began to cry, the excuse being, that my sister had hurt her finger.

In the evening another of my Mum's friends came to pick us up, whilst we were ready for bed. Very confused, we left, after an argument between two of my Mum's friends. We were taken to her house, where my Mum waited. She said that she and my Dad couldn't live together anymore, because they quarrelled.

I became very naughty. Then they decided to try again at their marriage, but one evening, while eating dinner, Dad called Mum darling, she yelled 'Don't call me darling, I'm not your darling'.

After repeating herself, my Dad apologised. He continued to call her darling, as he had done for fourteen years and it was habit. He eventually exploded, he ran upstairs and packed all his clothes in a big box. He cried whilst I screamed and pleaded for him to stay.

J became very difficult towards my Mum, as I believed it to be her fault at his leaving. I said how much I hated her and how horrible she was. I began telling her that she didn't love us. It upset her very much the way I acted, but she had custody of us. She decided to re-marry. We would have to move to Bristol. All I knew was that it was a long way from my Dad. I was very rude to my Step-dad and my Mum. I was only happy when I visited my Dad every other weekend. I kept up my bad behaviour for several weeks.

What motivated me to act like this
I acted this way, because I was confused. I felt I had lost something that I was close to. All I could think of was having a man, who I hardly knew, taking over from my Dad. Everytime I saw my Dad I cried. he shed tears too. Then he got married again, but although I was happy that he wouldn't be alone, he didn't seem mine anymore. I still feel that I have lost somebody that I love very much.

How I felt before and after
Before I let off all my steam I felt hurt and upset. I wanted to express my feelings, to let my parents know that I was there and to let me have my say. To tell them to think of us as well. After the incident I felt guilty at the way I'd treated my Mum. As I understood what was happening, and I was sure that I would still see my Dad I began to cope with the situation.

How the adult responded and the effect it had upon me
My Mum didn't hit me or tell me off, as she knew how I felt. She just tried to explain to me what was happening. My Dad said that it wasn't my Mum's fault, it was something they both decided on. Although I wasn't told off, I got very guilty and uncomfortable, knowing the way I had acted.

The way the adult coped with the situation and my comment
I believe my Mum handled this incident the correct way. I had been hurt, and my naughty behaviour was due to my confused mind. Frightened, as to what was going to happen made my anger worse. If my Mum had hit me, I would have been terrible towards her for a very long time. I was punished by myself. The guilt I felt afterwards, made me very unhappy.

Handicapped children

This is a study about handicapped children. The introduction gives some general information. The main part following is an account written by a student recounting how she learned about handicapped children. She monitors first a visit made to the class by a mother with a handicapped baby. Next she tells of a talk given by an expert who runs a centre for handicapped children, and finally describes her experiences when handicapped children are invited to a playgroup held by her class. The comments made about her own personal reaction as she acquired some knowledge about the handicapped child, and finally came into contact with some handicapped children, show the effect those experiences have had on her awareness and attitude to handicap.

Some types of handicap

There are handicaps which are hereditery, some which are congenital (happen in the womb), and some which can happen at birth, or can be caused by drugs, eg theledimide. Some handicaps can be caused by accidents, eg a car crash or an accident in the home. Some children may be quite normal inside but appear to be twisted and deformed, and some who are quite normal on the outside but are mentally retarded or have other defects.

Illness
Illness can cause handicaps, eg measles can cause deafness.

Parents
It is a great shock for parents to find they have a handicapped child. Parents almost always have a feeling of rejection for the child, but also feelings of guilt, and the feeling that it is their fault, or punishment for something they have done.

Mental handicap

What does the term 'mental handicap' mean?
Mental handicap is like other handicaps – for instance, wearing glasses. You are not ill and you cannot be cured, but you can be helped to minimise your disability.

Can I become mentally handicapped?
No, you cannot become mentally handicapped, but you can become mentally ill.

Do mentally handicapped parents have mentally handicapped children?
No, parents of all intelligence levels have chances of having a mentally handicapped child.

Can mental handicap be cured?
No. Mentally handicapped people will never be cured, but modern medicine is developing ways to prevent mental handicap, and we are learning to help and accept these people into our community.

Are mentally handicapped people dangerous? Should they be locked away?
Most mentally handicapped people are less aggressive than the rest of the population.

A description of specific handicaps
Mongol A mongol person has a broad face and sloping eyes. The official name for this is Down's Syndrome. This handicap is caused by a genetic error contained in the egg cell from the mother's ovary. People with this handicap usually make good progress with specialised teaching. A mongol child of eight will behave more like a three year old.
Autistic The word autism comes from a form of behaviour rather than a condition. Some autistic children are extremely gifted, and are thought to have a high level of non-verbal intelligence. Austistic children are very withdrawn and often take no notice of those around them. The cause of autism is not known.
Epileptic Most people who suffer from epilepsy are not mentally handicapped. Epilepsy is caused by minute damage to the brain. Drugs used by epileptics help them to lead as normal a life as possible.
Spastic Spasticity is the commonest form of celebral palsey. Many spastics are not mentally handicapped, about 50 per cent have normal intelligence. Spastics are handicapped because the part of the brain to function movement does not work properly. This means they have no control over their limbs. Sometimes the spastic's brain may be more affected and he may be severely mentally handicapped as well.

Spina bifida
Considering that conception and pregnancy is so complicated it is not surprising that development sometimes goes wrong. Usually most abnormal babies conceived end up as miscarriages but unfortunately some are born malformed. There are tests available to check on abnormal babies at around 14 weeks of pregnancy. This is called **amniocentesis**. A chemical test of the amniotic fluid can detect a substance which shows the foetus is not developing

properly and that the spinal cord is not completely closed over – a spina bifida with nerve damage. If this detected before the baby is born, the parents may be offered a termination.

EXAMPLES

A student's account of visit to class of mother with a spina bifida baby

Mrs Peel and Hannah

In June 1981 Hannah was born at the Royal Sussex County Hospital, Brighton, and was discovered to be suffering from spina bifida. Mrs Peel visited us on Friday 12 March and spoke to us about the birth, her feelings and life with a spina bifida child.

The birth and the discovery

The birth was a very long and tedious one for both of them. It lasted four hours, and Mrs Peel knew something was wrong, although after the birth no-one else knew anything was wrong, until after the photos had been taken and the doctors were doing the tests on the baby.

The parents' feelings

When the discovery was made Mrs Peel said many words rushed through her head such as: handicap, marriage, problems. Her husband thought the open wound on the baby's back was a birthmark, Mrs Peel said it looked like a wound with cling film over it. Things began to look even worse, after the tests the baby's legs were lifted up but they just dropped back down again, also needles were put into her legs but it made no impression on her.

The advice

The doctors and nurses advised Mrs Peel not to let the child have any operations – just let her die. So Mrs Peel took Hannah home and decided to let her have a normal, but short, life. Hannah was taken regularly to the hospital to check for head swelling. After eight weeks Hannah still hadn't died, so they decided to have the operations.

The future

Looking after Hannah is tiring and takes up all Mrs Peel's time. She has to change the dressings three or four times a day, and she will always have to be changed as she will never have control over her bladder or bowels.

Mrs Peel and her husband will have to be patient and extra loving, but I'm sure there will be advantages along with the disadvantages.

Pre-school handicapped children

Record of talk by Mrs Gould of the Jean Saunder's Centre
In 1971 the health education passed an act saying handicapped children should be taught. Up until then handicapped children were not taught at all. The Jean Saunders centre does this, it takes children from the age of two to five years (except in special cases when the parents really cannot cope).

The variety of handicaps at the centre are: spina bifida, mongolism, genetic disorders, cerebral palsy and microcephalitis.

First of all Mrs Gould is put in touch with the parents by paediatricians, health visitors or GPs. From when the baby is first born Mrs Gould visits the parents and baby, just to listen and talk and help get them through the first awful stage. Normally the parents have three stages of reaction – first they are in deep grief, as if they have lost a child. They cry and cry. Second they are angry and resentful and repulsed, 'Why me?' The third and positive stage, 'What can we do?' It is then that Mrs Gould can help them in looking to the future.

She visits and talks to parents, lending them the special toys they need. Mrs Gould also sets them tasks to do so they do not feel they are just wasting time. She also goes to specialists with them to listen to all the necessary information, as the parents do not always listen properly.

Then, when the children reach the age of two, they can go to the Jean Saunders Centre. We are very lucky to have one of these assessment centres in Brighton. The children go there from 9.30–2.30 daily. They are taught practical things how to use a toilet, table manners and how to act in everyday situations. The staff very much want to make the children feel normal.

Toys
The toys are varied. They use sand and water, puzzles, stationary toys. They also do music finger play, rhythm, and use climbing apparatus. All the toys are designed to combine hand to eye co-ordination. Each child is set a task for the day, continuation is very important. The staff child ratio is very good, each child has his own teacher. there are also trained physiotherapists at the centre.

Parents
Parents are welcome any time at the centre, but especially on Tuesday mornings when there is a coffee morning.

My reaction
At first I felt scared and embarrassed but then the feelings turned to guilt because I was normal and they were not. Then I felt sad. I never really know how to behave, I don't want to be pitying them, but it is mean and nasty to laugh.

I think centres like these are really great. I think it is very important not to shut these children away and pretend they don't exist.

When children like this are born I think it is completely up to the parents of that child to decide. It is not up to the doctor (although his advice is needed) and definitely not up to religious organisations. This decision is like the decision of whether or not to have an abortion – totally up to the people whose lives it is to do with. When babies are born very crippled and it is only machinery that is keeping them alive I think it is very wrong. Modern machinery and science are moving too fast for the human body.

Playgroup

Children from the Jean Saunders Centre

On Friday, the last day of the half term, we had some children in to a playgroup at school from the Jean Saunders Centre. About 12 children came in, most of them under the age of five. There were also lots of helpers from the centre who came as well because of the obvious difficulties involved in the travelling between the centre and the school.

Preparation

Because the children were handicapped, changes had to be made from the normal layout of a playgroup. We used two classrooms. One was layed out with refreshments and used for prams and coats, etc, while the larger room was used for play. All the usual toys were put out – sand, water, slide, wendy house and all the smaller toys, as well as PE mats were put in groups in places on the floor.

The children

The children and staff arrived at about 11 o'clock. The group that was before us saw to the refreshments, this was good as we didn't have very long with the children. When we arrived and the other group left we had to come into the classroom very quietly and slowly so as not to scare the children.

When I first looked the children looked just like other children. They were playing and were enjoying themselves.

Katie

The child my friend and I chose to play with was a little girl called Katie. Katie is two years old, and was big for her age. She was slim and quite tall with blonde hair and blue eyes. Katie's favourite plaything was a jigsaw puzzle, which she liked to put in her mouth and suck. Then we took her on the slide which she loved and had lots of go's. We also played with the sand, but she seemed very disinterested with it.

Katie didn't act as if she needed you there at all. She always kept her head down and would make no eye contact. She very much did her 'own thing' and just used you as a 'stepping stone'.

When I spoke to one of the staff about Katie she told me that the doctors didn't know what was wrong with her. She showed some signs of an autistic child, but was not one. She could not walk and her feet were a little deformed, although this would probably right itself. If you held her to stand, she would stand on her tip-toes. They also said that Katie likes to listen a great deal. The lady also said that she was glad that we liked Katie as people often did not take to her very much.

My reaction

I was determined not to be scared or repulsed by these children. I especially tried to remember what my teacher had said about them being just little children, (and just because they were a little different) and nothing else. I think this helped me a lot in understanding the children.

I did feel very upset when I saw the little girl who weighed under 400g, but over all I think the playgroup was a very rewarding experience, and I admire and think the people who work with these children cannot be praised enough.

Conclusion

Before our child-care group studied this topic on mentally handicapped children, I wasn't really sure what the differences were between mental and physical handicap and mental illness. Throughout this topic I have learned exactly what the differences are. I have learnt that these children are just normal, happy little beings, who want to lead a normal life. I feel that it is very important that they should be encouraged to lead a normal life and have a place in society just like everyone else.

Before we did this topic I always felt embarrassed and scared when I saw them. This topic has helped me a great deal in coming to terms with the fact that mentally handicapped children are just like other children. I think that if everyone had the chance to meet and play with these children like we did, then everyone would understand them, and not be so scared, a lot more.

Unmarried mothers

Reasons for becoming one

In our society where contraception is freely available and abortion is not against the law, women nevertheless become pregnant in circumstances which society would consider ill advised: they become pregnant without being married. True, women are no longer condemned to the work house or worse as in times past. Literature has documented very vividly the dire plight of such fallen women, you need but to read the description of Oliver Twist's mother's ordeal to get some inkling of what it must have been like. Nevertheless to become an unmarried mother is still a very difficult option: so why does it still happen:

Lack of love

Some girls get pregnant because as children they didn't have love and care from their families, they have always felt neglected and deprived of the one thing that all human beings crave for: love. Mistakenly they fall pregnant from a desperate desire to have someone of their very own to love them. Sadly they often find the reality of motherhood most difficult to cope with. They lack the emotional stability to respond to someone else's needs and become angry with their baby for not loving them enough.

These mothers can have problems with their children because they expect far too much from them. They are looking for what their children can give them, rather than what they can give their children. They might expect a child to do or understand far more than any normal child of the same age. The child will lack any warmth or security in his childhood because too much will be expected of him and he will be frequently criticised. Rather than having his varied needs met with consistent care, he will be forced to meet his mother's needs – when he fails he could become a 'battered child', thus continuing the cycle of deprivation and the same sad things that have happened to his mother will go on happening from one generation to another.

Through ignorance

Some women, even in this day and age, become pregnant because of ignorance of the 'facts of life'. They didn't realise that sexual intercourse actually causes a girl to get pregnant and they might also be ignorant about contraception.

Lack of control

Passionate and loving feelings are difficult to control and a couple can get carried away. Sometimes alcohol or drugs can distort reality and cause people to do things which without their influence they would not dream of doing.

Keeping a boyfriend

Love can make people behave in unpredictable ways. Women have been known to get pregnant when they realise the man they love no longer wants to know them, in the desperate hope that the child they carry will bind the man to them.

Relief from boredom – attention seeking

Young women in dead-end jobs, girls bored with school, women who are unemployed may decide to become pregnant to give their life a sense of purpose. They may enjoy shocking their families and surprising their friends and basking in the attention their situation will atract. Some may be mature enough to make good mothers, others may find bringing a child up on their own will make life even more restricting than it was before.

Bad example

Some girls may follow the example of their mothers or sisters who are feckless and careless with their morals and lack a sense of responsibility. It can be difficult for someone brought up in such an environment not to copy such behaviour.

Conscious decision

There are women, usually in their late twenties or early thirties, who are not married and who make a planned, conscious decision to become a mother. Frequently they are women with careers who feel they can support a child on their own.

Lesbians who have a stable relationship with another woman will sometimes have intercourse with a man in order to become pregnant. Sometimes they ask a doctor to arrange artificial insemination for them.

Rape

Women can become pregnant after they have been raped by a stranger or forced into having intercourse by someone they know.

Reactions of people involved

Possible reaction of the father

The reaction of course depends on the kind of person the father is, his relationship with the woman, his age and situation. Some men still respond in the age-old way of saying 'Are you sure its mine?' They react like this because they are afraid of the responsibility that goes with becoming a father. But it is, as it always has been, a hurtful and degrading thing to say to a woman, because it implies she sleeps around (a woman of loose morals). Another reaction is that the man feels very big and proud, so he may brag to his friends: 'Look at me I am a man, I've got a girl pregnant'. Other men will be caring and thoughtful. They will accept the pregnancy as a joint responsibility, which of course it is, and be prepared to support the woman and her baby.

Possible reaction of parents

All parents, particularly if their daughter is very young, feel very distressed when they are faced with the possibility of their daughter having a baby without being married. Often they feel that their daughter's situation is a reflection on them, that somehow they have failed in their role as parents. They may also be concerned that their daughter's reputation and theirs will be lowered in the eyes of their community. From a more mature and experienced vantage point they can see the effect the baby can have on their daughter's future. They may feel all their expectations of marriage and a career for her are now in ruins.

There are parents who react violently to such news, may attack their daughter and throw her out – others after reflection will do all they can to support their daughter in whatever decision about her condition she makes.

Choices open for the mother to be

Keep the child

The adolescents who become pregnant while they are still teenagers put a great extra strain on themselves, having a baby developing inside them while they haven't finished their own development. The pregnancy may undermine the health of both mother and child, particularly if the mother is not sensible about her diet or responsible enough not to smoke while she is pregnant. When the baby is born she is not very well able to look after him because she hasn't yet had enough experience at looking after herself. Frequently the father of her child is in a poor position to help her to take his share in parenting the child. In such cases the girl is often dependent on her mother for help. This means that she becomes even more dependent just at the time when she should be learning to be independent.

Any woman who decides to keep her baby will need support, emotional and often financial. Good organisation in these circumstances is essential for a single parent as there may be no one else to share in the tasks. It becomes necessary for most single parents to find a reliable minder and to be familiar with the support services offered by the state. The extended family, if available, takes on added significance, particularly to allay fears as to who would care for the child if anything happened to the parent.

For the child there may be confusion and conflict as it tries to understand why one parent is missing. It is usual for the mother in this situation to look to her child for support, such as she might expect from another adult. There may be a tendency to give the child adult privileges too early, discuss with them topics which they are not ready for – accelerate them into a role of adult companion too early.

Although it is a tough option, it is certainly possible for a single parent to bring their child up as a well-adjusted and happy individual and find fulfilment and a sense of real achievement from the experience.

Adoption

The mother gives birth to the child and the baby is placed through an adoption society with a couple who will adopt him. The mother loses all rights to the baby. There is a law now that assists adopted children when they reach 18 to trace their biological parents.

The mother can be secure in the knowledge that her baby has gone to a 'good home'. Prospective couples who apply for adoption are very carefully vetted before they are accepted as adoptive parents. The decision leaves the mother free to pursue her life and it must give her some satisfaction that she has made a childless couple extremely happy. Giving the baby up is of course very difficult for the mother, as it is her natural instinct to keep him, and it will create a void.

Placing the child in a foster home

Foster parents approved by the council could foster the child until such time as the mother has the means to care for him. She can maintain contact with the child through regular visits. The difficulties with this situation is that the child may become very attached to the foster parents and will become upset to leave them to live with his mother. Also foster parents can change and that is a very unsettling experience for the child.

Abortion

Abortion is not a possible choice for some women because it is against their religious beliefs or on moral grounds – they feel it is murdering a life.

Physical effects   It is a relatively simple surgical procedure, sometimes not even involving an overnight stay in hospital. There is a risk of infection after an abortion. Also multiple abortions lessen the chance of being able to conceive normally in later life. After an abortion it doesn't take long to get back to physical normality. The woman has an extended, heavy period, the effects of the anaesthetic have to wear off, and she may be a bit anaemic through loss of blood.

Emotional effects   The sudden jolt that an abortion causes the body upsets the hormonal balance and causes the woman to feel very emotional. Any woman who has an abortion should beforehand and sometimes afterwards have professional counselling. There is no doubt that the emotional recovery can take a good deal longer than the physical. Women can become haunted by complex and disturbing thoughts: they could feel guilty, become severely depressed, harbour feelings of worthlessness and doubt the justification for their decision. Unless they receive help, their future well being can be affected.

EXAMPLE

Asked to consider what qualities she would look for in adoptive parents a student wrote:

If I became pregnant, had the baby and decided that I wanted to have him adopted then if I could choose a family I think it would take a lot of time and thought. In a way maybe it would be better not to have the choice (in real adoption, you don't) because there are so many different sorts of people who want babies and I'm sure I'd keep on feeling I'd make the wrong choice.

The first thing I'd decide was that the people would be a 'normal' married couple. Although I don't think there is anything wrong with single people having children or gay couples adopting, I'd still feel that I didn't want my child to go to a home like that, although I'm sure it would be loved and cared for the same as it would be by a married couple.

The second definite thing I would choose would be a couple who could never have children of their own. I can't imagine how horrible it would be not to be able to have children and I think I would be devastated if I couldn't – so I'd choose a couple who couldn't and remember when the time came to give away my baby, how much joy I was giving to the childless couple. I think I would have wanted them to have been trying for a baby for quite a while, so I'd be sure that they really wanted one, about five years.

I don't think age would be a really important factor – but about 30 years. Financial status is really unimportant as well, but I think I'd want one of them to be employed, because unemployment can split people up. I'd want one of them to be prepared not to work and just look after the baby, I'd expect this because I suppose it's what I'd do. I'd want them to have a big family around them – parents, etc, because they might need support and help.

It is hard to say what the qualities of good parents are. They must not just love the baby but love each other as well and be prepared to understand what they are taking on when they have a baby. They must also be practical and know how to care for a child's both physical and emotional needs, but in a way that is what everyone learns as they go along and everyone will make mistakes but that is just part of life and the most expert of people make mistakes with children. For 'snobbish' reasons I'd quite like the couple to live in a nice big house with a garden, but it wouldn't really matter.

After deciding all this in the end there would be just as much chance of something going wrong in the marriage or things going wrong as if you hadn't picked. As long as the people genuinely want a child and can love and cherish it then that would be fine by me.

Child abuse

Children can evoke angry and violent feelings in anyone who looks after them. But what one does about those feelings is what really counts. One mother recalls that when she had such feelings towards her baby son, she would leave the room or think about all the good things about him: his sudden smile, his soft skin and lovely smell after he was bathed, etc. She also found two things reassuring, one was that she knew that other mothers felt the same and secondly she was aware 'how babies are sometimes, they cry and cry whatever you do for them'. She accepted her feelings as normal and did not take her anger out on her child.

There are, however, mothers, and in some cases fathers, who were themselves neglected and unloved, who are unable to sublimate or redirect their anger; they have no patience with any of the normal baby activities like crying, vomiting, spitting out food, dirtying nappies. A case reported in the paper described how a father bathing a baby was angered by the child's cries. He hit the child across the face, and when that only increased the child's cries, he held its head under the water, then lifted the child out of the bath and threw it down on the floor and kicked it across the bathroom. The dead child was placed in a cardboard box and left on a rubbish tip. Before this tragedy the father had confessed his feelings of aggression to the social services but they did not react quickly enough.

There are parents who pick on one child in the family and are reasonable parents to the other children. Perhaps that child wasn't planned, or was sickly looking at birth, and had to be separated from his mother because he needed nursing in the special care unit. Skinny babies are particularly at risk from violent parents because they are not cuddly. Other difficulties in the family become the focus for parental aggression and anger. Sometimes this 'scapegoat child' will remind the mother or father of themselves as children or he may have some resemblance to their own mother or father who had been cruel to them.

Children admitted to hospital with injuries which are suspected as being non-accidental are X-rayed. These injuries show differently from the normal falls that could cause them. Doctors and nurses will detect the tell-tale signs that the child is being battered and the social services will become involved and further investigations made.

Children who are ill treated by their parents rarely make dramatic gestures which would draw attention to their plight; they don't run away or show their injuries or plead for help. On the contrary, their loyalty to their parents is often very strong and they will go along with the false parental explanations of how their injuries came to be. They lack confidence to stand up for themselves and often feel that they deserve the ill treatment they receive, because they see themselves as being really 'bad'. After all, no one has told them any different, they are not to know that all parents don't treat their children in the same cruel way. They simply become mute with despair.

A register of 'children who are at risk' is compiled by the social services from information amassed from various sources; health visitors, doctors, teachers – any people who suspect that a child is being ill treated. The families are carefully monitored and help is given to them in the hope that they will become better parents and will not need to have their children taken from them into care. After the tragic death of seven year old Maria Calwell in 1973, who was brutally killed by her stepfather, procedures to help children at risk were much improved. The story of Maria is indeed very sad, she was in foster homes for the first six years of her life, where she was a happy loved and loving little girl. Her mother decided to demand her return. During the 14 months she spent with her mother, stepfather and brothers and sisters she was made to do hard work: carrying heavy bags of coal, doing the family shopping before she went to school, and she was subjected to prolonged ill treatment. A student I taught, who was in the same class as Maria, recalled how she had been away from school and when her mother took her back they discovered that the school was closed on that particular day. It was cold, a rainy day in late Autumn. At the school gate was Maria. My student's mother spoke to Maria and told her that she should go home as the school was closed for that day. The small girl, shivering in her thin clothes, explained that she had been back home but had been sent away again to stand at the school gates until the normal end of school day and there she had stood all that day, hungry and cold not daring to contradict instructions for fear of reprisals!

The National Society for the Prevention of Cruelty to Children (NSPCC) exists in order to help children who are in danger from their parents. Any one who suspects that a child is being ill treated can report their suspicions to the Society and investigations will be made. This Society estimates that 110 children are killed and 7,000 injured at home every year. Cruelty to children is a more common problem than most people would believe. A small number of parents who abuse their children are mentally ill, but most of them are fairly ordinary people, and none of us should turn our backs on such families and their children.

Violence in the family

Only in the last 28 years or so have people accepted that there is violence in the family, and that parents wilfully hurt their children.

Typical examples of violence, like broken bones, blood clots under the skin and fractured skulls were often dismissed as accidents and excuses, such as the child had fallen out of his cot or downstairs, were accepted. In 1955 an American doctor published an article which talked about parents battering their children. There are four kinds of child abuse:

1   Physical battering (hitting, pinching, etc)
2   Mental cruelty (making the child feel small and unimportant)
3   Starvation of: food, love and affection
4   Sexual abuse.

Baby battering
Baby battering can start with:
(a) *Separation of the mother and baby at birth*   The hours spent between mother and baby after birth are of vital importance and produce a special bond. If this bonding does not take place, then communication between mother and child can break down particularly if accompanied by other difficulties.
(b) *Feeding difficulties*   If a mother finds that the child will not take the feed properly she becomes very tense – this can often result in physical battering.
(c) *Constant crying*   A mother may become hysterical if subjected to constant noise and this can cause her to hit out at the baby. If a mother makes this mistake it is possible she may have the self-control to stop. But there are those who go on hitting the child until unconsciousness – or death – mercifully arrives.

Battering the older child
(a)   The child may cry if thwarted or contact is lost with the mother. This can aggravate the mother – and so her immediate reaction is to hit out.
(b)   Clinging and whining   When a child reaches a certain age he will become clinging and will whine – some mothers find this hard to cope with and find they cannot accept the situation. Other mothers may even find the dependence embarrassing and so the only way they can stop the child from whining and clinging is to hit out.

Most mothers control these problems but when major emotional difficulties occur it is difficult to keep cool!

Injuries inflicted on children

Some of the injuries children receive from battering are: Multiple injuries, eg burns, blood clots on the head, scratches, broken bones, marks from beatings, genital injuries, bruising, violent shakings, burns from cigarette stubs, and hair loss due to the child being swung by the hair. I once taught a small girl of six who had had bald patches over her head where the father had swung her by the hair as punishment for bed wetting.

Physical rejection and failure to thrive
Some of the ways parents neglect their children are to stop feeding them, which produces starvation. They will also stop changing the child which will lead to a sore bottom, and later pneumonia.

Neglect to older children
(a)   Parents stop feeding the child.

(b) If the child is a bed wetter some parents make them eat their feaces and change their own beds. The parents will also rub their children's noses in their urine -- just as they would an animal.

(c) Parents can have wrong expectations of children and this can come from inexperience. For instance they may give a young child a good deal of house-work or expect the child to look after younger children.

Mental abuse
Obviously mental abuse can be as serious as physical abuse. There are many types of mental abuse:

Excessive discipline

Isolation

Withholding affection as a punishment

Erratic management, ie inconsistent behaviour resulting in the child not knowing how to judge what is good or bad behaviour entirely because the parent expects a different attitude each time their adult mood swings.

Damages caused by battering
Battering can cause permanent damage or death. Some of the damages caused by battering are:

The child can actually stop growing or not grow enough

The child may become mentally retarded (brain damage)

The language development may be held up

The development of understanding may become stunted

The personality may become distorted

The child will find affection hard to show

The child may grow up to become a brutal adult because of being trapped what happened to him in childhood and the same sad things that happened to him will happen to his children.

Damage to the brain
Damage to the brain can cause:

Blindness

Deafness

Fits

Spastic body

Death

Children who are at risk
The children who are most at risk are:

Children who have been separated from their mother at birth because it is thought that the special bonding that occurs when the baby is first born is broken.

Children who are under two and a half years old because they are more likely to cry more frequently and are totally dependent on their parents.

Younger children – as they are more fragile.

Battering mothers are often pregnant or have just given birth because they are acting under stress.

There are usually more female batterers than male because the mother is with the child for long periods.

More injuries are inflicted on the child at home than anywhere else.

Reasons why parents abuse their children

Parents who batter their children have often been deprived of real parental love, affection and support from their own parents, for nothing is more contagious than an unhappy childhood. These parents expect their children to meet their needs. The parents don't see things from the child's point of view, and try to force them to see things from the adult's point of view. Some parents expect children to be slaves or servants to them and, generally, they expect *too much too soon*. They look for what their children can give *them*, rather than what *they* can give their children.

Parenthood does not come naturally

Parents sometimes expect more from a child than he can attain or understand. Parents expect *mothering* from the child, eg 'He should have known I was upset and kept quiet'.

Parents who have a low self-image find normal behaviour from their children unacceptable. They feel insulted and show their resentment in a combination of different ways.

Basically, parents abuse their children because they have had an insecure and unhappy childhood or have idealised, unrealistic expectations. Other reasons include the parent's own immaturity in age and emotional problems during pregnancy and birth.

Summary

All sorts of parents are potential batterers. They are unhappy people with many difficulties who need our understanding and our help to deal with their problems.

The problems which parents who batter their children have are a combination of the following:

Immaturity
Money worries
Worries about relationship with the opposite partner
Overcrowding at home
Lack of love and security in the parents life when they were children
Father's jealousy of the baby
Lack of understanding of the child's needs or behaviour patterns
Expectation of love from their baby to compensate for the lack of it from other people

Too high expectations of child, eg expecting the child to be 'good' and succeed – early potty training, walking
Too much emphasis on appearance, eg place too high a value on possessions – cleanliness, tidiness
Over sensitivity to what other people's attitudes are
The very difficult baby, ie early colic or rejecting parent and not responding to attention.

The parents' background
Unhappy childhood
No caring adults – no one to copy
May have come from violent families
They may have had rejecting parents
Parents who were: harsh disciplinarians, cold and distant or cruel.
    Mothers who have had severe depression after giving birth.

A way of informing the Social Services

Anna was asked to write a letter to the Social Services about a child abuse case. This is the letter:

Dear Sir
My name is Anna Williams and I am a teacher at Lakeside First School, Brighton. I am writing to inform you of a family I believe is in desperate need of help. I teach five to seven year olds, the remedial classes and there is one boy who has particularly caught my attention. His name is Jimmy Crabtree and he is six years old. He is exceptionally small for his age and very thin, especially around his face which is very hollow. His intellectual development seems to be stunted and even though he is in a remedial class he is way behind all the other children and shows no signs whatsoever of any reading or writing. He is extremely quiet and has no friends and finds it very difficult to participate in group activities. He frequently comes to school dressed in inadequate clothing and although the school office has supplied him with clothes many times he never wears them again and they are never returned. Jimmy often smells of urine which makes the other children reject him more. He usually has bruises on his arms and face and once one of my colleagues noticed that something looked wrong with his hand. He was taken to the hospital and it was found one of his fingers was broken and two badly fractured. Jimmy has a tendency to flinch if you move towards him and he is very un-co-ordinated.
    I have often invited Jimmy's mother to parents' evenings at school but she has never attended one yet. Jimmy's dad no longer lives with Jimmy's mum and she now has a boyfriend. Jimmy has two sisters, one nine years and from her marriage, and a two year old of whom the father is the boyfriend. Jimmy's mum (Mrs Crabtree) wanted to have an abortion when she discovered she was pregnant with Jimmy but Mr Crabtree wouldn't let

her. Soon after Jimmy's birth Mr Crabtree left so I think this could be one of the reasons why Jimmy is so rejected and neglected. The nine year old, Samantha, is left to do a lot of the looking after of Jimmy but obviously she is not capable of coping. The youngest child is treated reasonably well. They live in a high rise block of flats and both the adults are unemployed.

I have personally witnessed three acts of child abuse in the last three months. Samantha, the elder sister usually takes Jimmy home from school and brings him. Often Jimmy arrives at school much too early. Usually we bring him into school, but he has been known to be sitting in the playground at 7.15 am on a March morning. The first incident was when Mrs Crabtree's boyfriend collected Jimmy from school. It was raining and Jimmy didn't have a coat. At first the man was very rough and was walking very quickly so Jimmy couldn't keep up with him, when he crossed the road Jimmy ran to follow him and car narrowly missed him. This made the man very angry with Jimmy and he turned and slapped him hard across the face. Then he took Jimmy's wrist and practically dragged him along, when Jimmy stumbled the man turned and shook him violently. I often see Mrs Crabtree and Jimmy at the shopping centre. Jimmy is made to carry large bags of food that are much too heavy for him. Last Saturday afternoon he fell over and dropped his bag. His knee was cut yet Mrs Crabtree grabbed hold of him and hit him four times on the head. The third incident I witnessed was to his sister. I saw Mrs Crabtree push her out of the door of the flats and shut the door on her so she was locked out. This was in December when it was extremely cold. Samantha was dressed inadequately in a short cotton summer dress.

I now think it is crucial that the social services intervene. Recently Jimmy's injuries have been getting worse and if something is not done soon I think there could be permanent physical and mental damage. The incidents that I have witnessed are probably trivial compared to the agonies Jimmy is put through in his own home. Both Jimmy and Samantha are undernourished and neglected. Neither of the two children are thriving and Samantha is very unresponsive.

I think for their own safety both Samantha and Jimmy need to go into council care and then if the father was found and both parents gave permission for Samantha and Jimmy to be legally adopted, then I think this would be the best solution as both the children need some stability and real parental care in their lives. If adoption was not possible, then I think the children should be fostered, but kept together. Also, I think Mrs Crabtree needs professional help and if her problems could be resolved then maybe she could, with constant checks from the social services, perhaps have the children back one day.

I hope you will get in touch with me as soon as possible.

Yours faithfully
(Signed)
Anna Williams

Children in care

Children are placed in care to live in a children's home or a foster home because they need looking after. Their family arrangement having broken down, sometimes temporarily, sometimes permanently, the family may request that children be taken into care or children are placed in care because they are in need of care and protection.

Years ago children's homes were called orphanages, because most of the children in their care were children whose parents were dead. This is not so any longer.

There is more *divorce* now, and sometimes when one parent leaves, the other one finds they can't cope with the responsibility, eg have to go out to work leaving children with child minders, who let them down – older children may be left unsupervised after school and get into trouble with the police. Don't forget an unsettled situation at home will upset children and they will behave accordingly.

The same situation can arise if *one parent dies*. In the old days more people had extended families who would help out. Many people don't have this any more, and the social services have to step in.

Sometimes a *parent re-marries* and the new partner rejects the children who may in turn have rejected the step parent! The couple feel their only chance of staying together is to put the children into care.

Emergencies arise such as sudden illness – mental or physical, and children are placed in care. Parents might lose their home and children have to go into care until such time that the parents have somewhere suitable for the family to live together again.

Mothers occasionally get worn out caring for their family and need a break from the pressures, otherwise they would become ill; having the children in care for a time will offer Mum the necessary rest.

Occasionally *parents and children need a break from each other*. Family rows and tensions mount and it is better for them to be apart for a while.

There are of course those children who are *in need of care and protection*. Parenthood does not come naturally to everyone; children are demanding, noisy, messy, irritating and unpredictable and some parents will turn against their children, and ill treat them. There are parents who have a drink or a drug problem, which makes their behaviour completely irresponsible.

Years ago there were many children who were homeless and who spent their lives in the streets with no one to take care of them. In some parts of the world it is still true today. They usually form small gangs with a leader, beg or steal food and live rough. Many die early and some take to drugs or prostitution. In England *Doctor Barnardo* came to London and was so appalled by the wretchedness of those children that he raised money and opened homes for them where they would be cared for and educated. The money came from private donations, but it is now the responsibility of each local council to care for children who have no one of their own.

Each child in care has a social worker attached to him who has his best interests at heart. At six-monthly intervals, all the people responsible for a child, review the child's situation to see if anything needs to be done, eg if he is not getting on with a set of foster parents or if he is doing badly at school, they will look into the causes to see if anything more can be done for the child. The child can refer to his social worker himself if he has a problem. Unfortunately social workers get married, move away or change their jobs and children lose continuity. Some people feel that children in care need more representation, and moves are being made to give them a special 'spokesman'.

To conclude this section on children in care I include two very revealing and moving accounts of childhood experiences written by a student who herself was in care. She was one of five children whose mother rejected her, she spent time in a children's home and was fostered for a time with her aunt's family.

EXAMPLES

Students recalled their own experiences of being in care.

Information

I was living with my cousins Beverley and Mandy as their Mum had adopted me when I was about five.

I wasn't the youngest because my cousin Beverley was a year or two younger than I was. I got on well with my cousins and I called my auntie 'Mum', but I never asked where my real Mum was because I was sent to a home when I was young before I went to my auntie and cousins.

The incident

As I hadn't been living with my auntie very long, she kind of spoilt me, and Mandy, who was about four years older than I was, didn't like this. She was a jealous girl and she definitely knew how to hurt somebody.

My 'Mum' had gone out and she brought us all a new toy. Beverley had a small doll, Mandy had a purse and I had a make-up kit, which I used to do my dolls up with.

Mandy didn't like her purse but liked my make-up kit because she thought it was more grown-up.

When I was using my make-up kit on my dolls, Mandy came up to me saying, 'I hate you. You get everything. My Mum doesn't buy us any nice things anymore, now you're here. I wish you hadn't come into this family.'

I ran into the bathroom and locked the door. During that time I was in the bathroom Mandy had smudged the make-up on my doll's face.

When my Mum called us down for our tea I didn't go. She came up and knocked on the bathroom door. 'I'm not coming, I'm not wanted', I remember saying. When I unlocked the door, my Mum could see that I had been crying and asked me what I was crying for. I told her and she was furious. She had a word with Mandy.

How I felt

I felt very unhappy, hurt and out of place for quite a few days, because I couldn't get those words out of my head, and when I went to bed I used to cry because I always thought, whoever I went to, nobody would want me and I would be out of place all the time.

Mandy regretted what she had said to me and would not stop saying 'Sorry'. After that we were all right together and I didn't tell my Mum that Mandy had ruined my doll, because I could see that Mandy was very upset, and I didn't want to get her into any more trouble.

How the adult responded

My Mum settled me down and told me not to worry because they all loved me.

She told Mandy and Beverley they would not be left out of anything, she only wanted to make me feel wanted and at home, and she didn't realise that Mandy didn't like the purse.

My comments

I agree with what my Mum had done and I think it was a good idea for her to talk to us on our own, so that we would both understand. It would also have been a good idea for Mum to buy us the same things as each other so that we would not be jealous.

The incident

It happened when I was having a party with my dolls because my cousins were out and I was with my foster Mum and Dad.

I had this so-called party joyfully in the front room. I bought sweets and my Mum gave me some cakes and biscuits for my party. I was playing quite happily on my own when my cousin Beverley came in and asked if she could play. I let her play because she had a little black doll I liked and if I hadn't let her play she wouldn't have let me play with her black doll.

When all of the food had gone Beverley went and played on her bicycle. My Dad had come in and I had set all my dolls up on the table and it took me a long time. My Dad came over to say hello and he knocked my dolls off the table and one of the doll's heads came off. It was my very best doll which I took around everywhere with me. The doll's name was Susie. My Dad did say sorry but because I was only six I could not be without that doll. I would not sleep but when I did sleep I kept on dreaming about my doll. It was a nightmare because the doll kept coming towards me without any head.

The next day when I was with my cousins, I went into the rabbits' and guinea pigs' cage which my Dad spent a lot of time with, and let them out and left the shed door open so that they could escape. I went upstairs and played with the other dolls in my pram. When my Dad came in he said hello to us all, had his tea and went to feed his rabbits and guinea pigs.

He came storming in and said, 'My rabbits and guinea pigs are gone. Who knows anything about this? They must have been let out.' I immediately said, 'I never. It wasn.t me, honestly,' but my Dad knew it was me.

How I felt

I felt scared and frightened because my cousins had said to me whatever you do to us, or to anybody else, we will do to you. So I didn't want to tell my Dad in case he shut me out all night.

The only reason why I had let the rabbits and guinea pigs out was because he broke my doll's head off, so I wanted his rabbits' or guinea pigs' heads to be chopped off too.

How did the adult respond

When my Mum went out that night, and my Dad looked after us because he didn't want to go out, he was tucking me into bed and he said to me, 'I am not accusing you of letting out my rabbits and guinea pigs but I have the feeling it was you because you immediately answered it was not you.'

My Dad understood why I had done what I did and offered to buy me a new doll but I wanted my old one.

My comments

When I realised what I had done, I felt sorry for the rabbits and the guinea pigs but I was really pleased that my Dad hadn't done the same for me.

Summary

Devising and teaching this course has been for me a journey of self discovery, it has also shown me that we can come to terms with, rather than become the victims of, traumatic childhood experiences which to some degree none of us escape. Too often when we become adults we create a barrier which prevents us accurately interpreting the true logic that motivates the actuality of a child's actions. It has been very exciting to witness pupils on this course being able to respond to children without the restrictions of such a barrier, and to see them grow towards maturity. I do believe that the approach to the study of children outlined in this book inspires a commitment, an understanding and an acceptance of children which can only bode well for the future.

Index